WHEN gods CHANGE

D0916063

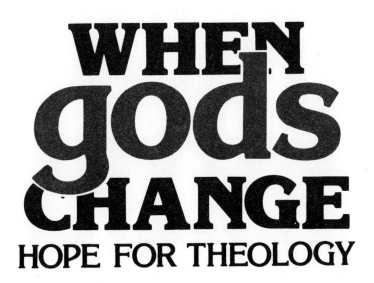

WHEN gods CHANGE

HOPE FOR THEOLOGY

CHARLES S. McCOY

ABINGDON
Nashville

WHEN GODS CHANGE: HOPE FOR THEOLOGY

Copyright © 1980 by Abingdon

Library of Congress Cataloging in Publication Data

MCCOY, CHARLES S
   When gods change.
   Includes bibliographical references and index.
   1. Theology—20th century. 2. Pluralism (Social sciences)
   3. Liberty. I. Title.
   BT28.M24   200'.1   79-27890

ISBN 0-687-45001-2

MANUFACTURED BY THE PARTHENON PRESS AT
NASHVILLE, TENNESSEE, UNITED STATES OF AMERICA

FOR

MARGIE

CONTENTS

PREFACE

God and the gods have always been humanity's most vexing problem. Every affirmation humans make in understanding themselves and their world reflects their ultimate convictions. Every action they take emerges from their most comprehensive commitments. The key, therefore, to the shape of human community, to the contradictions of human existence, to the conflicts in meaning and value, to social cohesion and division, to the realities of oppression, and to the possibilities of liberation is to be found in the plural gods of human believing.

Given the centrality of deity for human living, why is the entire spectrum of theological studies in such turmoil today? It seems, to paraphrase W. B. Yeats, that theology is falling apart, that no center of faith will hold. This situation ought not to cause surprise. To the extent that believed-in gods are the summation of human misery and hope, there will always be commotion and confusion in theology.

Rather than speaking only of a theology of hope, therefore, we should ask: Is there hope for theology? When we look at the procession of theological fads over recent decades, the answer to that question cannot be an easy yes. There is no hope, I am convinced, for theologies

11

mired in the past, insulated from human suffering, and isolated from wrestling with real oppressions. There is hope if theologians undergo the travail of emergence from ecclesiastical and academic wombs, cease talking mainly to each other, and contend with issues shaping human society and history.

In times of cultural ferment, when the gods are changing, stress and strain are inevitable in human believing. Some forms of theology will disappear, but not theology. Reflection on believed-in deities will continue to provide one of the surest means for understanding the human condition.

In the chapters that follow, I hope to throw light on the perplexing scene of religious faith and reflection and the forces shaping it. In Part 1, pluralism and the globalization of culture will be explored as the *context* of changing patterns of human believing and theology. In Part 2, the notion of shift in paradigms provides a *perspective* from which to understand theological transformation and the role of change in religion. In Part 3, liberation understood within a covenantal paradigm will be proposed as central to a transformed *method* in theology and ethics.

Certain convictions inform my thinking and may be helpful in understanding my argument. First, there is today widespread and disabling confusion about the nature of human believing. Some seem to think that faith is a form of knowledge rather than the fiduciary dimension of all human knowing. In a parallel misunderstanding, gods appear to be classified at times in the same series as rocks and anxieties rather than as the most comprehensive of multiple levels of commitment and meaning. Many persons not involved in those simplifications view comprehensive meanings and values as human "creations," while regarding the "everyday world" as "real." In the perspective offered here, our various provinces of meaning, as in a federal republic, are symbiotically interdependent. The everyday level is no less dependent on the wholeness that gives it shape and definition than the wholeness depends upon its parts. Covenantal or federal epistemology offers a persuasive alternative to the idealisms, positivisms, and their successors in the Western intellectual tradition.

Second, I am convinced that theology and ethics have significant roles to play in the continuing quest for justice, equality, and love. This belief runs counter to much that theologians say about their own work as well as what is often assumed among those who suppose they have nothing to do with theology. Pluralism and liberation, as powerful cultural forces today, are disclosing the theological dimensions of all human action and communities.

Third, only a transformed theology, I am convinced, can come to grips with the emerging situation in global culture. The theological pattern dominant in the Western tradition—a pattern I shall call the Constantinian paradigm—is too narrow in scope to deal with the contemporary plurality of faiths, values, and interests; with the diverse movements of human liberation; and with the expanding spheres of human interaction.

In no sense does this mean that I wish to discard the Western theological heritage. It is our past, my past. Instead I dwell within this heritage which is my own, not to repeat its formulations like magical incantations, but to break out into the widening world of contemporary culture. The context of ethnic pluralism in the United States and impetus toward liberation around the globe, for example, appear to me to be more certain clues to the future shape of theology than do the ecclesiastically and nationally isolated theologies of Europe and North America. Black preaching and theology, with their reliance on biblical story and dramatic recital, offer a more creative direction for theological development than linguistic analysis and hermeneutical esoterics. Action and agency provide a more comprehensive focus for theology than do words and symbols. The covenant of God presents a more biblical, and more persuasive, view of "process theology" than do the derivative versions dependent upon recent metaphysical systems. And the emerging global culture requires attention to the diversity of human believing rather than to facile dichotomies like "belief " and "unbelief," "sacred" and "secular," or "faith" and "religions." These preferences of mine draw deeply on the biblical Christian heritage but constitute a rejection of the limitations imposed by the Constantinian paradigm.

My debts are heavy and many, but none of my creditors in faith and reflection ought to be held accountable for what I have done with their contributions to my thinking. The influence of H. Richard Niebuhr, Robert L. Calhoun, and Paul Tillich, with whom I studied, will be especially apparent. In the longer heritage of human thought, I draw upon Plato, though not with the conventional misunderstanding of him as idealist, upon Johannes Cocceius and the stream of federal thought of which he is the most eminent theological representative, and upon a community of interpretation informed by Charles Sanders Peirce, William James, Josiah Royce, and George Herbert Mead. Michael Polanyi taught me new ways to understand philosophical reflection in relation to theology and ethics. Among my contemporaries, Martin Luther King, Jr., Jürgen Moltmann, Elisabeth Moltmann-Wendel, and Benjamin Reist have influenced me by their example, friendship, and theological pioneering. Marjorie Casebier McCoy, my partner in love, continues to teach me in all ways the meaning of faith and hope and love. My participation in the Christian community since earliest childhood and in movements for human rights since high school provides my human location, shapes my interpretation of past, present, and future, and gives me the faith by which I understand God and my companions on this journey through life and history.

The materials making up the pages that follow have taken form in classes in the Graduate Theological Union, in presentations at the Wilshire Boulevard Jewish Temple, Los Angeles, and at the Pastoral Conference of the Pacific School of Religion, Berkeley, and in lectures at

PREFACE

the Universities of Tübingen and Münster in Germany. Discussion in all these settings has contributed to what is now appearing in print.

My sister, Rosemary M. Lemmond, did much of the typing of the final manuscript. My daughters, Sherry and Stephanie, helped with proofreading. Tom Wolfe assisted with the proofreading, with the preparation of the index, and with the checking of citations. To all these persons, I express my gratitude.

Charles S. McCoy
Berkeley, California

OVERTURE

THEMES OF DEITY

So Paul, standing in the middle of the Areopagus, said:
"People of Athens, I perceive that in every way you are
very religious."

Acts 17:22

The times change and with them so do the gods of
humanity.

Ludwig Feuerbach

I.

THE DREAM

In my dream, I was taking a poll for a social science research center, asking people about their religious beliefs. In one hand I carried a clipboard, in the other a pencil.

My task was to ask persons a single question: "Do you believe in God?" On a sheet attached to my clipboard, I was to tally the responses in one of three columns: Affirmative, Negative, Uncertain/No Opinion. The job seemed straightforward and uncomplicated—ask the question, note the answer.

Looking around for my first respondent, I found myself on a mountainside. The vegetation on the craggy slope was scrubby and sparse. Stones jutted out of the reddish gray soil. As I surveyed this desolate scene, my gaze fell on a man sitting on a rock at the entrance to a cave. He was very thin, with skin burned dark by sun and wind. A single garment of animal fur hung loosely on him. His hair and beard were disheveled, his manner disconsolate.

I approached him ready to ask my question, but he took no notice of my presence. He was gazing toward the sky with great intensity. I started to speak, but before I could begin he cried out in an agonized voice, "What am I doing here? Surely, O Yahweh, you know!"

He paused and glanced wildly about the bare landscape. I realized with astonishment that he was actually addressing deity.

"You know that I have been very jealous for Yahweh, the God of Nations," he continued. "But the people of Israel have been false to your covenant. They have destroyed altars dedicated to Yahweh, killed your prophets, and run after other gods. Now only I am left in all Israel as a believer in Yahweh, God above all gods. And they pursue me to take my life."

I looked around nervously to see if we were about to be attacked but saw no one else. My mind churned with confusion. Could I actually be in the presence of Elijah, prophet of the redeeming, liberating God of Israel? This was an opportunity that I must not miss. I grasped my clipboard and pencil more firmly and stepped forward boldly to ask my question.

Suddenly, the calm was broken by a wind of gale force with lashing rain. The ground shook as in an earthquake. Pieces of rock rushed past me. Lightning flashed around us, and peals of thunder followed.

In a short time the disturbance subsided. The man was now crouching with his ragged mantle flung over his head to protect himself from the elements. Gradually his face emerged, and he peered out intently as though listening to the silence.

Taking advantage of the lull, I stepped toward him and called, "Elijah, Elijah." So violently did he start that I paused.

"Don't be angry with me, Yahweh. Being a minority of one is not easy." He stopped speaking and seemed lost in thought—or hearing something beyond my senses. Abruptly, he rose to his feet and stood up straight. "So I'll go back and face down the people, the false prophets, and their gods," he shouted, shaking a fist toward the sky. "But if I survive the fury of the baals, O Yahweh, I expect a replacement."

Then he took off running down the barren slope.

I pondered the matter a moment and decided that

Elijah ought to be listed in the Affirmative column, even though I had not succeeded in getting a direct answer to my question from him. I began to feel that my task was more complicated than I had thought. As I raised my clipboard hesitantly to record Elijah on my response sheet, the scene dissolved before me as though washed away by a final gust of rain.

A city square paved with uneven stone blocks took shape around me. In front of me was a marble building with a porch and a roof supported by columns. To the right, not far distant was a high hill with a familiar-looking temple on it. With a shock, I realized it was the Parthenon, whole and magnificent on its hilltop site. I was standing in the Agora looking upward at the Areopagus and Acropolis of ancient Athens.

Shaded from the bright sunlight on the porch of the marble building, a group of young men surrounded a bearded oldster, who appeared to be speaking with one member of the group. Could it possibly be Socrates engaged in one of his famous dialogues?

As I considered whether to interrupt them or wait until their animated conversation was finished to ask my question, a youth emerged from a narrow street to my right and started across the Agora toward the group around Socrates. Stepping up to him briskly, I spoke in my best interviewer's voice, "Pardon me, sir. I want to ask you a question." He paused and looked at me curiously. "Do you believe in God?" I asked.

A puzzled look came over his face. He glanced at Socrates and then back at me. Perhaps he thought I was only asking troublesome questions. He could not know that I was engaged in important scientific research. I held my pencil poised, ready to tabulate his response in one of my three categories. My alertness and sincere expectancy seemed to overcome his doubts.

"Well," he began slowly, "some gods I believe in and others I'm not so sure about." A bit of animation appeared in his face. "At the Temple of Athena, we have excellent seminars in logic and rhetoric. Eventually I hope to receive a diploma certifying me as a sophist and lover of wisdom. I really believe in Athena. But then Socrates raises difficult questions about sophism and some of the gods." He paused.

I looked at my clipboard, wishing there were more than three alternatives. It sounded as though he might belong in each category, depending on which god was being discussed.

Looking back at him, I discovered that his countenance had suddenly begun glowing. "This evening," he said enthusiastically, "I'm going to the Temple of Aphrodite. You might want to go with me. First, the priestesses dance and chant before the altar. Afterward there are fascinating activities in the gardens. At first I was afraid and uncertain but then I became liberated. Now I really believe also in Aphrodite." He stopped suddenly, and his face darkened. "But I do not believe in the god of war and . . ." He began a catalogue of gods he rejected.

I ceased listening and looked at my tally sheet in despair. Just in time to save me from my quandary, the Agora became a concrete shopping mall in some city in middle America, whether Dubuque, Fresno, or Manhattan was unclear. At least, it was a setting more familiar to me.

The clipboard was still in my hand. My goal was a hundred responses, but that did not seem many for the mall was filled with people going about their business. Surely I could get my work done now. I went patiently to work, accosting respondents, repeating my question, being endlessly pleasant, attempting to make the answers fit the three categories.

A tall eagle-eyed man lectured me on the dangers of asking such a question, which was obviously of the devil and could sow doubts in the minds of believers. A plump, older gentleman assured me that God and religion were fine if they did not interfere with business or politics. One lady glared at me as though she suspected I had made an indecent proposition, but assured me that she did believe in God once I shouted the question loudly enough for her to understand. Another woman replied with a surprised,

"Of course," as though unaware of any alternative. A man snarled curtly, "Hell, yes." Those could be tallied in the affirmative. Less clear was the intelligent, friendly woman who assured me that religion was wonderful because it fostered great art. I was even less certain how to classify the poker-backed man who thought churches helped produce law and order and the white-haired fellow who talked at length about being a regular churchgoer, liking the music, feeling "recharged" by worship, but never answered my query. The vague, attractive girl who responded with a puzzled, "Who? . . . What?" followed by a coquettish, "Well, maybe," I tallied in the uncertain column. And the precise young man who stared at me with lifted eyebrows and answered, "Heavens, no," I counted as negative.

When at last I had coaxed responses from a hundred persons, I tabulated the results: eighty-seven had given more or less affirmative replies; six had responded somewhat negatively; and seven had seemed uncertain or confused. I had accumulated the information, but the results failed to get at the varied gods of the respondents. I remembered Elijah and the multiple deities of Athens.

Shaking off my doubts, I lifted the clipboard ready to make my report. But it slipped from my grasp, hit the pavement, and shattered. Liberated from the puzzles of my dreaming, I awoke, staring into the bright light of dawn. Though still confused, I was at least clear that better ways must be found to investigate the varied patterns of religious believing.

II.

THEOLOGY IN TRANSFORMATION

After Pablo Picasso had completed a portrait of Gertrude Stein, she complained to the artist that the picture did not look like her. Picasso merely smiled at her and replied, "It will. It will."

Many persons practicing in the field of theology will examine the portrait of their discipline as I shall depict it here and complain, as did Gertrude Stein, that it does not resemble at all what they understand themselves to be doing. My response to them, like Picasso's to Stein, is, "It will. It will."

Dramatic changes are taking place today in theology. How are we to understand and interpret these changes? What is the significance of change itself for Christian faith, for religious communities around the world, and for theological reflection? I hope to throw light on these questions and in the process to suggest new perspectives on the meaning of pluralism and liberation for theology, on the relation of faith and knowing, and on the nature of human believing.

Though it is not clear that a majority of theologians in Western academic centers recognize the sweeping changes under way in religious thought, a perceptive few are aware of them. "The first thing to be said," Jürgen Moltmann has written, "is that theology is today undergoing a great transformation."¹ One of my Berkeley colleagues, James W. McClendon, Jr., asks, "Where are we now in theology?" and replies, "A shift is in progress. The old landmarks set by Barth and Rahner, by Tillich and Congar, are slipping away, or perhaps the changing countryside makes the old features unrecognizable. What seemed so durable when the present generation was in school may appear quaint or incredible."²

Rosemary Ruether is even more explicit. "The scope and method of theology are going through a striking transformation in the present era," she writes.

Theology is losing its confinement as an exclusively ecclesiastical science, but only because it is finding its place in a reintegrated view of the human community. It is losing its place as the science of a particular ecclesiastical tradition or even of a single historical faith, such as Christianity, but only because it is beginning to glimpse its place as the horizon of a human history that is truly catholic. It is losing its place as a science confined to the sacral of the "religious" sphere, but only because it is finding its place within the totality of human activities and the arts and sciences that reflect on and create these activities.³

If this analysis is correct, the change now in process does indeed involve transformation of a profound and sweeping nature. No longer can theology be assumed without critical reflection to be a function exclusively of the Christian church or of some particular Christian sect. The incredibly loose way that Christian theologians in Europe and North America have often used the terms "theology" and "Christian theology" as though they were synonymous must cease. In the same way, theology is also moving out of its academic isolation and entering into fruitful relations with the entire spectrum of intellectual endeavor.

When examined carefully, the theological transformation now taking place is far more significant than the shift in emphasis from Walter Rauschenbusch to Reinhold Niebuhr in America or from Adolf von

Harnack to Karl Barth in Europe. It involves a more fundamental change in method than that from Augustine to Aquinas. It means an even greater alteration in theological method than the one that took place in the Reformation of the sixteenth century. This transformation involves the displacement of the basic pattern that has informed and guided most Western theology since Augustine, and its replacement by a paradigm that places theology in a global context of pluralism and liberation. This means fundamental change in the methods, concepts, and language of theology.

To glimpse the magnitude of the theological transformation now taking place, we must compare it with the momentous shift in theological method that produced the dominant Western paradigm. Contrast Plato's use of the term "theology" as stories about gods in the *Republic* (379A) with its rational meaning in the *Summa Theologiae* of Thomas Aquinas. Or set the biblical language of historical recital, metaphor, and parable alongside the discursive argument in Calvin's *Institutes* or Barth's *Church Dogmatics*. It required a great transformation to change from story to rational disputation as the basic pattern of theology.

A change of similar proportions is now in process. Contrast Reginald Garrigou-Lagrange's *God: His Existence and Nature* or Eberhard Jüngel's *The Doctrine of the Trinity: God's Being Is in Becoming*, with works exemplifying the transformation: H. Richard Niebuhr's *The Meaning of Revelation*, Martin Luther King, Jr.'s *Stride Toward Freedom*, Kosuke Koyama's *Waterbuffalo Theology*, and James McClendon's *Biography as Theology*. In such comparisons the transformation can indeed be perceived.

The pattern that has informed most of the Western theological tradition is in process of dissolution, and a new pattern is emerging to replace the old one. The traditional pattern can best be described as the Constantinian paradigm. With variations, this Constantinian paradigm has dominated Christian thought in the West since the time of Augustine. Thomas Aquinas followed this pattern. The Reformers continued it with revisions. Schleiermacher and Barth, Bultmann and Rahner, adhere to it, as do most persons working in theological faculties of the North Atlantic nations. The same conventional pattern has influenced the entire spectrum of religious studies and popular thinking about religion. Now the Constantinian paradigm is cracking. A theological revolution is taking place.

To understand the conditions requiring this transformation, it is necessary to recognize that we live, not in a time of the twilight of the gods or the death of God, but rather in a time of the reappearance of the gods and the manifest liveliness of God. The fears of theologians that religion and theology are fading away derive from the theologians' insularity. In the world outside sectarian and academic enclaves, it is a time of the dawning of new and multiple deities, a time when isolated religious communities are being drawn out of themselves by a globalization of culture. It is a time when the reality of religious believing is inundating the rational methods of the Constantinian paradigm. It is a time of changing gods and changing theologies.

1. Change and Continuity

To say that change is taking place is not to say that change is always and unequivocally good or that the means for measuring and evaluating change are simple. Even as we recognize the transformation occurring in theology, we must also emphasize the importance of continuity within the change.

To no small degree, the vagaries of theology in recent decades resulted from the tendency of theologians to embrace *either* change *or* continuity as though they were mutually exclusive. Avant-gardists seem always to think that what is "new" or on the "frontier" is by some magic rendered better than what is old and central. Their counterparts, the traditionalists, hold to the reverse formula: if it is ancient and settled, then it must be better. Francis Cornford, the great classical scholar, often said that a university is a place where nothing is ever done for the first time. If that be so, then theology of the rigidly traditional variety is uniquely suited to reign as queen of the static sciences.

Yet a third group may now be emerging. It is composed of those who have entered serially into every theological craze of recent decades and now propose to throw themselves into another fad: orthodoxy. This new fashion has characteristics similar to earlier ones: enthusiasm, simplistic labels, and neat dichotomies. In this latest example of theology à la mode, we are called to choose between orthodoxy (good) and heresy (bad), between classical Christianity (good) and modernity (bad), in short, between continuity and change.

We need not regard ourselves as authentically alive only when we are in a perpetual state of future shock, wrestling with innovations and breakthroughs. Ordinary routines and repetitive activities, those most obvious reminders of continuity, must be given ongoing attention. Neither is it required that theologians or human beings generally become merely curators of the musty museums of the past. Living involves the continuing integration of tradition and innovation into the freshness of every present. Theological reflection partakes, therefore, as much of continuity as of change. Relating the inherited past to the emergent future ends only with the end of all our histories. Utilizing the resources of tradition to meet the challenges of new situations is the difficult task of human believing and of theological reflection in every here-and-now.

How are we to relate change and continuity today? How are we to be faithful to the heritage given us by our own community of interpretation and still be responsive to the present context of global pluralism and rising aspirations for liberation? Let us look at theological change in the light of these questions.

The Constantinian paradigm emerged in the early

centuries of Christianity from the efforts to be faithful to a Hebraic past yet responsive to a Hellenistic culture saturated with Graeco-Roman religions and philosophies. At the same time, the Christian movement grew from the faith of a persecuted minority to become the faith of the emperor and the empire. Out of this meeting of continuity and change came a momentous innovation—the Constantinian paradigm for Christian theology.

As it has come to dominate Western theology, the Constantinian paradigm may be characterized as follows:

1) It has assumed and accepted the dominance of organized Christianity in society. This ascendant position was achieved in the fourth century, consolidated in the Middle Ages, and maintained until the twentieth century. The Reformation principle, *cuius regio, eius religio,* represents no more than a variation on this aspect of the Constantinian paradigm. As a consequence, religion has tended to be defined across the entire spectrum of religious studies in terms of institutionalized Christianity. The reduction of religion to this conventional form has caused unending difficulties in dealing with religious pluralism with reference to world religions as well as the alternative faiths present within Western society, outside ecclesiastical institutions. Even the disestablishment of Christian churches has done little to alter this Constantinian assumption.

2) The Constantinian paradigm assumes that theology is restricted to the ecclesiastical sphere and regards theology as the function of a particular ecclesiastical enclave. Theologians formulate the convictions of a single community and interpret the world in terms of those formulations. The community governing the work of a particular theologian may be Roman Catholic or Protestant, Lutheran or Anglican, Presbyterian or Baptist. It may also be national, so that its theology is that of the British Anglican Church or of the German Evangelical Church. Whatever may be their differences, Friedrich Schleiermacher in *The Christian Faith* and Karl

Barth in his *Church Dogmatics* begin with the conviction
that theology is a function of the Christian church. And,
of course, each means tacitly that sector of the Christian
church to which he belongs. Theology within the
Constantinian paradigm is ecclesiastical theology.

(3) The method and style of theology within the
Constantinian paradigm is borrowed from one or another
philosophy. Augustine depended on neoplatonism,
Aquinas on Aristotelianism. Luther's thought depended
heavily on nominalism, but Lutheran orthodoxy lapsed
back into reliance on scholasticism. Protestant theology
since 1800 has usually been Kantian of an idealistic or
existential variety, while Roman Catholic thought has been
almost exclusively neo-Thomist. Contemporary theologians not only follow the rationalistic and discursive style of
the traditional paradigm but also do not seem to think it
possible to do theology without relying on some particular
philosopher. With this dependence on philosophy has
come also acceptance of the bifurcations presupposed in
the Western intellectual heritage—subject/object and
subjective/objective; essence/existence and substance/
accident; noumenal/phenomenal and theoretical/practical.
For theologians who follow the conventional pattern,
theology must be philosophical theology.

4) In the Constantinian paradigm, theology is proclaimed in the "imperial mood." Theologians assume that
they occupy a transcendent perspective, an ontological
peak, outside and above the limited perspectives of
historical and social location. Rudolf Bultmann can write,
"It seems to me that Jaspers claims to have attained a
stand-point as a philosopher outside of history," and soon
thereafter adds, "In faith, the Christian has the stand-point
above history which Jaspers like many others has
endeavored to find."[4] Faith is turned into some kind of
knowledge, and the believer is turned into God. To be sure,
philosophers and physicists, historians and social scientists often adopt the imperial mood in their utterances.
When they do, they are unconsciously following the
Constantinian paradigm of Western theology.

WHEN GODS CHANGE

Theological transformation is necessary because existing cultures are breaking out of their isolation and a new culture on a global scale is emerging. The horizons of human communities are no longer limited to a specific geographical area or ideological "tribe." A common realm of meaning and communication is taking shape across old boundaries and around the world. By radio, television, and film, through travel and cultural exchange, the horizons of young and old are being widened. Blue jeans are worn and rock music is heard in Hamburg, Tokyo, and Berkeley. World news is reported in London, Buenos Aires, and Cairo. The language is different, the emphasis varied, but the events and meanings are increasingly similar. Human culture is becoming global in scope.

Over the past century, the emerging globalization of culture has placed increasing pressure on the Constantinian theological paradigm of the West. Confrontation with other cultures in the missionary outreach of Western Christendom has raised difficult questions. The appearance of various so-called secular movements within Western society has presented a tangle of unresolved issues. The ecumenical movement has breached the walls of traditional ecclesiastical enclaves. A vigorous Marxism has challenged the socially conditioned theologies of North Atlantic societies. Ecclesiastical theologians are confused by wider cultural horizons and fearful of the diverse deities and plural theologies now appearing on the global scene.

As pressure on the Constantinian paradigm has grown, attempts have been made to modify it. Nineteenth-century liberal theology in its varied phases tried to accommodate the paradigm to the emerging cultural situation, to relate to the proliferating academic disciplines and the plurality of cultural forms. The efforts of liberalism, however, did not do justice to the element of exclusivism in the biblical heritage, and a vigorous neo-orthodoxy arose to oppose and largely displace liberal theology. Adolf Harnack, spokesman for the liberal tradition, viewed the task of theology as one with that of all sciences. Karl Barth opposed him with an abrupt *nein* and proclaimed the task of theology as one with the task of preaching.

Barth and neo-orthodoxy triumphed, but the victory was shortlived. By the 1960s, neo-orthodox theology had made its point and was receding. The reason for its early demise is not difficult to discover. Its rejection of liberalism, accurate in many ways, was too comprehensive. Though it retained the critical spirit, neo-orthodoxy rejected the culture-encompassing impulses that had been a major strength of the older movement. Looking back on their exchange, we see now that Harnack and Barth were correct in what each affirmed and were in error only in thinking their views totally antithetical. In any event, neo-orthodoxy tended to cut theology off from creative movements in the surrounding culture and from relation to the emergent diversity of global culture. The result was increased stress and strain within the Constantinian paradigm.

If this be so, then the strange assortment of theological fads of recent decades comes into focus. "Demythologizing" and the "secular theology," the "honest-to-God" and the "God-is-dead" movements, etc., disclose in their inadequacies the problems of Constantinian theology. Changing cultural conditions and a new religious situation are dissolving the traditional paradigm and pointing to the emergence of a transformed theology.

2. Metaphors of Transformation

Over the past century investigations into the microcosms hidden within the realms of physics and biology have opened new worlds and new problems for humanity. Behind the ancient notion of the atom the richness and variety of sub-atomic particles have emerged into view. Within the biological cell, the mysteries of human life are unfolding. Such pioneers as Willard Gibbs, Marie Curie, Albert Einstein, and Niels

WHEN GODS CHANGE

Bohr in physics and Charles Darwin, Gregor Mendel, James D. Watson, and Francis Crick in biological science have discovered these new worlds, and with their findings have come new challenges to theology and ethics. Now the emergence of a pluralistic culture on a global scale is compelling us to embark on another exploration into the richness and variety of human meaning behind the ancient macrocosmic notion of God. Rather than exploring the workings of electrons, positrons, and neutrons, the goal of this latter quest involves exploring the patterns of comprehensive commitments shaping human action.

In order to understand the shifting shapes of human believing and the transformation now taking place in theology and ethics, I shall utilize two central metaphors: (1) changing gods, and (2) covenant.

The first of these, changing gods, serves several purposes. It illumines the context of pluralism in the emerging global culture. On the one hand, the metaphor directs attention to the diversity of religious believing and the changes that are taking place in the direction and character of human loyalties. On the other hand, the image of changing gods underscores an aspect of the plurality that each faith tends to overlook: that persons of other religious beliefs believe, not in illusion, but rather in what they understand to be reality. The metaphor also illumines and provides countervailing impulses to the tendency of much theology and ethics in the Western tradition to presuppose a static deity. A metaphysic of divine stasis, with its corollary notions of unchanging substance and eternal essences, has become increasingly unsatisfactory in articulating the biblical Christian view of reality or the sense of dynamism that permeates most spheres of human experience in this century. Still further, the metaphor emphasizes the importance of human location in the study of horizons of commitment, with reference both to those who are the subject of such investigation and to those who are the investigators. It becomes much more difficult to suppose that intellectuals generally or persons with a "right" philosophy or a "critical theory" occupy an ontological peak outside history from which they can view reality and describe truth.

For the theological tradition in which most Western theologians have been trained, the notion of changing gods is strange. Indeed, it may appear to many thinkers to be impossible or contradictory. In some interpretations, it is impossible even to speak of multiple deities or plural faiths.

The most simplistic form of this Western theological perspective informs sociological research holding a Western, static conception of deity. As a result the question, Do you believe in God? is dubiously applicable to Elijah's Hebraic context, irrelevant for the world of Socratic Athens, and inadequate to explore the ordinary experience of middle Americans. What can it mean to speak of changing gods?

First, and most obviously, the phrase directs attention to the plurality of gods in which human beings have believed and continue to believe. Within the Judeo-Christian tradition we believe in the deity designated as the God of Abraham, Isaac, and Jacob, the God of Jesus Christ (some interpreters of Jewish tradition remind us that this formula points to the different believing in God of each of these patriarchs). The horizons of human believing, however, extend beyond that tradition. Other communities believe in other realities, other gods.

Second, given this plurality of deities, it is possible that a given person or community can alter the direction of believing from one god to another. Changing gods, therefore, can mean conversion. The traditional theological paradigm makes room for conversion from "unbelief " or "paganism" to Christian (or perhaps Jewish) faith or for "losing" faith and becoming an "unbeliever." The notion of plural and changing gods illumines what is ignored or perceived imprecisely in conventional theology: that the so-called unbelievers also believe. A wider world of believed-in gods is opened for theology as is the possibility of investigating with inclusive thoroughness the religious dimensions of human living.

Third, the notion of changing gods reminds us that God as believed in within a particular tradition may change rather than remain static. There is, to be sure, continuity within the biblical Christian tradition. When we examine the development of that tradition, however, it becomes clear that the understanding of God has changed over the centuries and with shifting locations— from Abraham to Moses; from Amos to Second Isaiah; from the Old Testament to the New Testament; from Augustine to Thomas; from Luther to Lutheran orthodoxy; from Asia to Europe, to America, to Africa, and back to Asia; from the affluent nations to those faced with internal need and unrest; from "white" theology to "black" and "red" theology. Christians may affirm that the God in whom we believe is unchanging, but we have no perspective outside the shifting patterns of historical location from which to speak of that deity. The notion of changing gods can aid in overcoming idolatrous fixation on limited and limiting conceptions of God.

To make this point of change within a particular tradition vivid, let us look at a contemporary example of change with reference to deity. In the Judeo-Christian heritage, God has long been referred to as male. Masculine images like "father" are deeply rooted in our liturgical tradition. We routinely use masculine pronouns for Yahweh. Some theologians have defended the notion that a male deity requires an exclusively male priesthood. Not all theologians appear to have noted it, but our conception of God is undergoing dramatic and visible change in this decade. The male image for God is being widely questioned and often rejected. The female aspects of the biblical deity are being lifted up. The prominence of women in our heritage is being given renewed emphasis; for example, the Gospels are unanimous in saying that the first proclamation of the resurrection of Jesus was entrusted to women (Matt. 28, Mark 16, Luke 24, and John 20). We are beginning to speak more accurately of the God of Abraham and Sarah, of Isaac and Rebecca, and of Jacob and Rachel. God is changing from a man into a deity combining masculine and feminine elements and transcending both. In the Christian tradition, before our very eyes, deity is undergoing change.

Fourth, if change in the pattern of believing within Christianity (or within other religious communities) were not disturbing enough for the older paradigm, there is the even more disquieting possibility to which changing gods points: that the God in whom we believe is changing rather than changeless, in process rather than static. Perhaps God may be better understood as moving target than as unmoved mover. Encounters with Marxism have contributed to the recovery of this possible perspective on biblical deity. Creative movements in contemporary theology are teaching us to think of God in terms of promise and fulfillment, in terms of eschatology and hope, in terms of process. God may be drawing us into the newness of futurity rather than holding us back in an unchanging past. For many it is discomforting even to imagine a situation in which we live amid changing gods. It is still more difficult to entertain the possibility that a notion of change in deity may enable us to be more faithful to the God of Christian faith.

The second metaphor is that of covenant. This notion, rooted in the Bible and Christian history, makes it possible at the same time to stand in continuity with the biblical Christian tradition, to anticipate change, and to absorb new emergences within the scope of that tradition. To make full use of the metaphor of covenant requires that we recover an important part of the Christian heritage that has been neglected and largely forgotten—the covenant or federal theology. This stream of Reformed thought informed varied sectors of the Christian movement in Europe and North America. The covenant is also an important and continuing motif in Jewish thought. In particular, the federal theology provided an indispensable means for moving from the protest of Reformation to the political and economic patterns of modern democracy. Embodied in the religious and social heritage of the United States, the covenant has shaped our federal institutions but has been ignored, I suspect, because of a pervasive "colonial mentality" among North American theologians. This mindset has led them to attend to theological and historical interpretations from Europe rather than to elements of their own heritage, which might prove more illuminating, not only of American society, but also of Europe and the world in this time of pluralism and the globalization of culture.

Together, the metaphors of covenant and changing gods enable us to envision a new paradigm for theology and ethics. In this paradigm, liberation is no longer a subsidiary theme or a possible result but rather a central theological principle by means of which God and divine action in history, sin and salvation, ethics and human responsibility, the church and eschatology are to be interpreted.

3. Transformation in Christian Perspective

As the Constantinian paradigm dissolves and theological transformation proceeds, what does it mean for Christian faith and theology?

First, transformation in theology will remind us in our believing as Christians that we continue to occupy a human location rather than a "transcendent" one. In the Christian community, we have come to trust Jesus Christ as the Way, the Truth, and the Life. This does not mean, as some apparently assume, that we have suddenly left our human location in a particular history. All this may seem too obvious to say, but the writings of Christians contain enough lapses from a wholesome awareness of our humanity that continuing reminders are needed, especially for theologians.

Second, transformation will remind us that Christian

faith is *faith*. In the expressions of Christian faith, we are not making statements that have some "objective" claim to Truth. Faith has not been transmuted into knowledge. We are not claiming to have achieved an Archimedean point of power or infallible insight. Such a view would be idolatrous. We are confessing our faith and seeking in our confessions and our action to be true to that sovereign reality we have come to trust through Jesus Christ. Being true has more to do with faithfulness and unfaithfulness in terms of a covenant than with spoken or written statements about some static, metaphysical Truth. To be sure, Christian faith is faith in God and not faith in faith. But again, this has to do with our faithfulness and unfaithfulness, our loyalty and our disloyalty to One we trust to be faithful.

Third, transformation will bring back into Christian theological awareness the multiple gods of human believing. The world is not divided into believers and unbelievers, as theology informed by the Constantinian paradigm holds. The unbelievers also believe, and they are committed to their gods. In a fit of forgetfulness, Western theologians have frequently overlooked the obvious context of diverse deities in Old and New Testament. Recovering this insight enables theology and ethics to understand with greater precision the context of human believing in the world around.

Fourth, transformation will recover the impulse toward saga, story, and parable prominent in all major religious traditions and especially significant in the Hebrew and Christian scriptures. The paradigm which has informed Western theology tends to discount the importance of artistic narrative in favor of dogmatic formulations shaped by philosophical notions of precision and truth. As a result, the theology of Europe and North America has not only become excessively rationalistic in its language and standards but has also become mired down in a bifurcated world of Western philosophy. Theology within the emerging paradigm will not reject philosophy, but it will be governed in form and language more by Jeremiah, Jesus, and Martin Luther King, Jr., than by the dogmatic style set by Thomas Aquinas, Johann Gerhard, and Karl Barth.

And fifth, transformation will help restore a sense of mystery to God as believed in by Christians. Christian faith and theology are recovering the Hebrew reluctance to give a final name to deity. Perhaps also we can recapture the willingness to follow God trustfully through the perils and suffering, the diversity and change of human history. Christians still are like Abraham and Sarah, who go out in faith, not knowing where they are going (Heb. 11:8). Yet the activities and worship in the churches seem organized to insure that nothing new or unanticipated will ever happen again. And biblical studies and theology usually seem to be carried on by "scribes and Pharisees" more intent upon defending themselves against the intrusion of anything new than witnessing to the unexpected, mysterious ways of the Risen Lord, who is making all things new.

In this perspective, the notion of changing gods in no way betrays Hebrew-Christian monotheism. On the contrary, it helps restore continuity with the covenant God and recover a vital awareness of the interaction between the historical realities of human living and the ultimate mystery of deity, the interaction between the shaping power of the past and sovereign newness of the future. The covenant God of historical promise and fulfillment is revealed in the changing patterns of human loyalties and believing.

We need not, however, await a distant future to see theology in process of transformation. We can see signs of change and illustrations of transformation in many places, though no single example contains all the elements mentioned above.

In their own way, the bizarre theological fads of the sixties point toward transformation by disclosing the serious problems within the ecclesiastical paradigm. Elements in the late work of Karl Barth and Paul Tillich suggest an awareness that momentous changes are under way. Among Roman Catholics, the work of Bernard Lonergan and Hans Küng most decisively exhibits currents of transformation. Among Protestants, process theology reflects some aspects of the changes taking place. The writings of the Japanese theologians, Kazoh Kitamori and Kosuke Koyama, illustrate Asian contributions to transformation. In philosophical work important for contemporary theology, we see striking new elements parallel to those mentioned above in Ernst Block and Michael Polanyi.

The fascinating attention to story and narrative as sources for theology that begins to appear in the seventies exemplifies an important facet of the transformation taking place. Essays by James McClendon, Robert McAfee Brown, James Cone, Heinz Weinrich, Ulrich Simon, Dietrich Ritschl, and Hugh Jones illustrate this trend.

We see transformation at work in ethnic theology—in the sermons of black preachers, in the speeches and writings of Martin Luther King., Jr., in the theology of the Native American movement, and in the brilliant treatment of ethnic theology by Benjamin Reist. The work of theological change can be seen also in feminist theology, especially in Rosemary Ruether and Letty Russell.

Jürgen Moltmann, probably the most influential theologian of the past decade, illustrates elements of the transformation of theology in his work. He writes:

From first to last, and not merely in the epilogue, Christianity is eschatology, is hope, forward looking and forward moving, and therefore also revolutionizing and transforming the present. . . . The world is full of all kinds of possibilities, namely all the possibilities of the God of hope. Faith sees reality and humankind in the hand of the One whose voice calls into history from its end, saying, "Behold, I make all things new," and from hearing this word of promise, it acquires the freedom to renew life here and now and to change the face of the world.[5]

WHEN GODS CHANGE

Most clearly of all, we see the pattern of a transformed theology and ethics emerging in the work of H. Richard Niebuhr, increasingly acknowledged as one of the most important religious thinkers of this century. Niebuhr names three central convictions that inform and transform Christian faith and thought:

The first is the conviction that self-defense is the most prevalent source of error in all thinking and perhaps especially in theology and ethics. . . . The second idea is that the great source of evil in life is the absolutizing of the relative, which in Christianity takes the form of substituting religion, revelation, church or Christian morality for God. The third conviction . . . is that Christianity is "permanent revolution" or *metanoia* which does not come to an end in this world, this life, or this time.[6]

In all three, he strikes at the core of the Constantinian paradigm.

Niebuhr's emphasis on the confessional form and historical method of theology was both ahead of his time and also a recovery of a vital element of the Christian past. He saw clearly that his approach requires that the heart and controlling shape of Christian theology derived from "the story of our faith."

Yet what prompted Christians in the past to confess their faith by telling the story of their life was more than a need for vivid illustration or for analogical reasoning. . . . Their story was not a parable which could be replaced by another; it was irreplaceable and untranslatable. . . . We find that we must travel the road which has been taken by our predecessors in the Christian community. . . . We must do what has been done because we have discovered with Professor Whitehead that "religions commit suicide when they find their inspiration in their dogmas. The inspiration of religion lies in the history of religion." Whether this be true of other faiths than Christianity we may not be sure, but it seems very true of our faith.[7]

And the telling and retelling of the story of our faith continues to revolutionize our believing, convert the patterns of our action, and transform our theology and ethics.

Because it is no longer adequate for the emerging cultural situation, the obsolescent Constantinian paradigm is breaking. The hegemony of scholasticism in Roman Catholic theology is fading. The dominance of neo-orthodoxy in Protestant theology is disappearing. The globalization of culture is well under way, and a paradigm for theology is taking shape for which pluralism and liberation are central.

Johannes Brahms, when asked why he waited so long to publish his First Symphony, responded, "How could I publish it with the footsteps of the giant so close behind?" Movement toward a fundamental transformation in theology is now taking place and will appear with increasing clarity as the footsteps of the theological giants fade.

PART ONE

CONTEXT: PLURAL GODS AND GLOBALIZATION OF CULTURE

For my thoughts are not your thoughts,
neither are your ways my ways,
says the Lord.
For as the heavens are higher than the earth,
so are my ways higher than your ways
and my thoughts than your thoughts.

Isa. 55:8-9

As there thus seems to be no one elementary religious emotion, but only a common storehouse of emotions upon which religious objects may draw, so there might conceivably also prove to be no one specific and essential kind of religious object, and no one specific and essential kind of religious act.

William James

III.

PLURALISM AS PROBLEM AND POSSIBILITY

"The world's a ship on its passage out and not a voyage complete," writes Herman Melville in *Moby Dick*. This image provides a perceptive summary of the human experience in the twentieth century. Characteristic of our time is an acute awareness that we exist between an uncertain whence and an unknown whither. We live under way, on the move, in the midst of mystery. Yet, as Melville's metaphor reminds us, it is not a situation that empties the present of meaning. Every present is laden with the remembered past and anticipations of the future. As we seek *logos* in *mythos,* our uncompleted voyages are filled with memories, with hopes, with partial understandings, and with inescapable believing toward unseen horizons of mystery and ultimate reality.

The image of humanity on a voyage is not new. The consciousness of being in midpassage, between darkness and darkness, is among the oldest views of human existence. What distinguishes our own era of existing *in medias res* from other periods is the pluralism emerging on a global scale and the challenge with which that pluralism confronts humans on every level of living.

Pluralism manifests itself in part today as societal diversity. In the multiplicity of nation-states and blocs of nations, in the economic and political groupings within nations and across national borders, in ethnic and sexual consciousness, the plurality of society intrudes into the boundaries of our awareness. This diversity is countered by strong pressures toward conformity, yet the confusing plurality remains.

Pluralism appears also on the psychological level. We are pulled in different directions by the appeal of diverse and often conflicting loyalties. Caught in the midst of these pressures, we seek for individual and collective identity and, in the process, experience identity crises as the plurality threatens to overwhelm us. The excitement of diversity and the newness in our world stimulates us but is counterbalanced by the perils of alienation and schizophrenia.

Pluralism exhibits its presence too on the cultural level of human experiencing, in the multiplicity of ultimate values, meanings, and faiths. East and West encounter one another with differing views of what is the best life-style and what achievements are to be valued most. Communism confronts the free world, not only with military threat, but also with the challenge of different social patterns and goals. The insecurities of the Third and Fourth Worlds disturb the relative comfort and material well-being of the First World. In the sweep of their influence around the globe, major religions come into contact and competition in an emerging marketplace of world views. Pluralism permeates the entire fabric of contemporary living.

The focus of attention here will be on the implication of this multifaceted pluralism for religious faith and theology. And conversely, we shall be concerned with the light that theological reflection throws on pluralism. My approach from the perspective of theology and ethics is not accidental. I have chosen it because I am convinced that the exploration of religious believing in its dimensions of valuing and moral action as well as of meaning offers the most comprehensive way to understand and relate the varied strata of human living. Ultimate convictions, as they emerge from religious traditions and faiths, shape cultural horizons, pervade the inward experiencing of persons, govern actions and relations in social interaction, and define the interests that bind ecclesiastical, political, economic, ethnic, and other societal groups together. And in providing coherence, such convictions also divide social groups from one another.

In this perspective it is clear why God and the gods always prove to be the crux of human problems, though self-deception, the facades of positivistic metaphysics, and theological confusion often conceal the pervasively religious dimensions of human living. The problem of God appears in ordinary guises and extraordinary disguises. By what criteria shall we act and order the priority of goals and values that inform our action? What loyalties and meanings capture our highest commitments and provide us with a sense of significant identity? What can we rely upon as real and enduring? Where can we give ourselves in love and find ourselves loved in return? These questions haunt us now and have always been sources of a strange combination of frustration and fulfillment for humans. And all are "religious" questions, with the answers revealed and concealed in the deities humans believe in. Issues at the core of existence, those most important for humanity, when traced to their roots, are grounded in that sense of value and reality signifying believed-in gods.

Within a remembered past and an anticipated future defined by our deepest and most pervasive convictions, human living in every present takes shape and finds significance. Around the still turning point of final faith, humans discover who they are, act in legitimated patterns, and affirm the criteria by which they understand justice and love. In these ways, religious faith and tradition are primary sources of the human sense of location and orientation; as pluralism has emerged and had its impact on the psychological levels of humans seeking individual and collective identity, on the societal level of groups seeking recognition and rights, and on the cultural level of personal seeking for ultimate meaning and faith by which to live, it has been recognized increasingly as a problem for humanity of the most profound sort. Specifically, the challenge of pluralism to religious faith must be acknowledged as a challenge to what is most fundamental and at the same time most pervasive in human living. As such, pluralism cannot fail also to have a disquieting effect on theology and is considered by many to be a mortal peril to the entire religious enterprise. Human believing in its most intense forms is the primary locus of social belonging, of personal identity, and of cultural orientation. Because believed-in deities are the focal forces of human living, the meeting of plural communities with their divergent views of ultimate meaning raises questions for religious faith and is a significant challenge to theological reflection. As I shall seek to make clear, however, pluralism when understood with care and precision presents not only problems but also possibilities for theology.

1. The Changing Meaning of Pluralism

From the perspective of historical awareness, meanings are not static but change with the passage of time and with shifts from one social or cultural context to another. Meanings alter also with linguistic shifts, with changes of political and national location, or with alterations in social relationships differentiated by ethnic, class, and economic status. As one example, we may consider the successive transformations in meaning that have occurred in biblical faith as it has passed through differing socio-cultural contexts; the problems of interpretation are further compounded by the shifts in its expression from Hebrew to Greek, to Latin, and then to the wide variety of modern languages.

Pluralism both points to this changing character of meaning and is itself also subject to change. As our experience of cultural diversity has extended into the past and around the globe in the present, pluralism has developed new meanings. Contemporary treatments of pluralism frequently do not take account of its changing significance. Indeed, many authors either presuppose some limited meaning or fail to make clear exactly what they take pluralism to mean. There can be neither clarity nor precision about the significance of pluralism for us today without a serious attempt to dispel the confusion and distinguish the emerging meanings of pluralism.

At the basic level of understanding, we must keep in mind a fundamental distinction. Pluralism can refer: (1) to a condition of plurality or diversity, or (2) to an attitude toward diversity, an interpretation of the variety, or a theory affirming plurality. Perhaps it would have served the interests of clarity if the word "plurality" had been maintained to designate the first meaning and the word "pluralism" reserved for the second. But usage has gone beyond that point, and now we can only attempt to distinguish the two.

Though both meanings can be traced back to the ancient world and into Eastern societies, it is in the modern world that they have entered the general fabric of culture rather than remaining the insights of a sophisticated elite. The ability to perceive plurality in the human community, rather than regard others as inferior versions of ourselves, is no small achievement. As this perception has been heightened and extended by the many encounters with societal and cultural diversity in recent centuries, pluralism has become more deeply imprinted in the everyday consciousness of humanity. And as pluralism has become more generally perceived and diffused, its meaning has grown and become more complex.

Pluralism, for example, may be viewed as a philosophical doctrine. As philosophy, it is to be contrasted with the ancient metaphysical monism of the *Upanishads* and Parmenides or with the modern monism of Spinoza, Schelling, or Hegel. Philosophical pluralists like Leibniz, James, and Russell hold that reality is made up of a multiplicity of principles or entities. A gentle pluralist like William James writes, "The pluralistic world is thus more like a federal republic than like an empire or a kingdom."[1] Bertrand Russell, with a harsher doctrine known as logical atomism, can affirm, "The most fundamental of my intellectual beliefs is that [monism] is rubbish. I think the universe is all spots and jumps, without unity, without continuity, without coherence or orderliness, or any of the other properties that governesses love."[2] Building upon the work of Charles Sanders Peirce, Karl Popper, and Paul Feyerabend, Helmut Spinner has developed an intriguing perspective which he calls "fallibilistic pluralism." He develops a doctrine far more complex than the sharp alternatives presented by James and Russell, even as it has greater kinship with the view of the former.[3] Philosophical pluralism has been developing and changing.

Pluralism may be viewed also as a societal and cultural phenomenon. As it has become a part of the emerging sense of history over the past two hundred years, pluralism has enabled us to recognize the varied perspectives that belong to differing human locations. Gradually we have learned to perceive with greater precision diverse patterns of social organization, cultural meaning, and religious believing in civilizations of the past and among other peoples of the present. In the process we have become more conscious of the convictions that distinguish our own community of interpretation and have come to see that persons living in other communities are not merely "strange" or "different" but have a perspective of their own. They too belong to a community of interpretation with actions, customs, and beliefs that have an internally coherent structure of meaning. Humans from other cultures may behave in ways that seem peculiar from our perspective. They may fumble around and make mistakes when they enter our cultural sphere and attempt to deal with our customs and our grammar. But we now understand that they are not necessarily stupid in their own language.

WHEN GODS CHANGE

As the implications of cultural pluralism emerged, many assumed that it necessitated the adoption of a relativistic view of all meaning. If some people believe one thing and others another, then no viewpoint could lay claim to any truth. On this basis, a general fear of pluralism has arisen, especially among those who cling to the social and religious past. But, as our understanding of pluralism has grown, a further insight has developed. It is not necessary to agree with the views of other communities in order to recognize that their folkways, social forms, and religious convictions have a coherence and integrity from their perspective and that the participants in those communities really believe in the cultural meanings and beliefs that are theirs. Even though we accept the plurality of socio-cultural systems, we are not required therefore to take any particular view of their truth or error, either in a proximate or an ultimate sense. We may recognize the plurality and regard all, none, one, or some combination as true. Pluralism does not entail relativism. As we shall see presently, pluralism may be regarded in one sense as the antithesis of relativism.

Now a further extension of the meaning of pluralism appears to be developing. Foreshadowed in the awareness of diverse faiths and multiple cultures, given impetus by developments in pluralistic philosophies, especially as these have worked themselves out in the social sciences, this new meaning has been shaped by intensified ethnic and sexual consciousness. It has appeared with special clarity in the United States but is rapidly becoming the experience of persons and communities around the globe.

The American colonies were settled first from Europe and acquired early a diversity representing the many nations and varied religious enclaves of Great Britain and the Continent. The Native Americans formed a part of this plurality, though the whites took their land, pushed them back across the wilderness, and almost extermin-ated them. Soon enslaved blacks, brought forcibly from Africa, joined the increasingly rich mixture on the American continent, with later additions from Asia and

50

Micronesia and further waves of immigration from Europe. The wide variety of ethnic groups that converged on the United States came for different reasons, but they did not come together in that new nation without inequities or without the age-old tendencies of human groups to exploit one another. The early arrivals from Europe tended to dominate American society, exploiting the blacks and the later arrivals from Asia and Europe. This dominant group shaped the American heritage and expected all the diverse ethnic groups to accept this history as their own. Though there was intense pressure to conform, the ethnic enclaves refused to become fully homogenized. The varied ingredients that found their way into the American melting pot did not melt. As a result of this refusal by ethnic groups to become absorbed into an amorphous whole, the plurality of American life has developed increasingly toward an innovative heterogeneity.

From this situation of stubborn ethnic resistance to amalgamation, a pluralistic society of sorts has been emerging. The civil rights movement has raised the struggle to public view. The emergence of a women's movement, seeking liberation and equal treatment, has added new dimensions to this pluralism. But what has come out of the struggle is the clear demand that diverse groups be allowed to participate in all sectors of society on an equal basis without giving up ethnic and sexual distinctiveness and without conforming to a dominant cultural pattern. In wrestling with this situation, the meaning of pluralism has been extended and changed.

In addition to its metaphysical-philosophical meaning and its cultural meaning, pluralism has come to mean also a societal situation in which a variety of groups with different ethnic, racial, religious, and sexual consciousness maintain their own identity, develop their own traditions or special interests, and participate in a common society from their own distinctive perspective. And as a still further extension of its meaning, pluralism has come to mean policies or doctrines that advocate or support societal pluralism. Though this form of pluralism can be discerned in the policies of Alexander the Great, it is emerging anew in more independent and stable form.

With this development being so prominent an element in the United States, it is not surprising that some of the most innovative and influential thought, utilizing pluralism as a central principle, has arisen in the United States. Charles Sanders Peirce and those influenced directly by him—William James, Josiah Royce, John Dewey, and George Herbert Mead—represent the mainstream of this intellectual movement. Reinhold and H. Richard Niebuhr represent it in the field of theology.

The ethnic revolt against homogenization, however, probably plays a more important role than do intellectual forces in shaping the awareness of plurality that is emerging, namely, that human differences of culture and faith can be affirmed rather than feared. We are learning that love of our own country need not blind us to the beauty of other skies for those who dwell beneath them. Out of an American experience, enlarged by global travel and encounter, Harvey Cox may be reaching toward this understanding:

Speaking English does not preclude my learning to talk in French and perhaps learning to understand a little of several other tongues. Indeed, learning another language frequently helps us to learn the limitations of our own and to appreciate its positive qualities more. This is also true of faith. In addition, as one hears and learns more languages, one discovers that the human reality they encode and express is shared by all people. But one also finds out that the variety of human languages is not just an inconvenient misfortune; it reminds us that there are actually multiple forms of consciousness, and that no single thought-word system could possibly encompass the infinite ways reality can be grasped and symbolized.[4]

Different communities have distinct histories, diverse gods which shape their memories, their loyalties, and their hopes. While we may not be able to see how this diversity can be reduced to unity, we may draw on the resources of our different communities to accept the multiplicity of ethnic, racial, religious, and social groups. Perhaps we can even come to affirm plurality and to strengthen political and societal patterns based on less than ultimate agreement. The United States has been compelled by stubborn, irreducible social forces to fumble its way toward a form of such a pluralistic order. The federal political philosophy and the partial separation of church and state have been important elements in this development. At best, the American example is only a beginning. But it is a beginning that is being duplicated in other societies and is becoming transnational in scope. It is possible that a new humanity is moving uncertainly and haltingly toward a similar pluralism on a global scale.

2. Threat to Theology?

As pluralism has emerged in its global setting and had impact on the psychological level of humans seeking individual and collective identity, on the societal level of the oppressed seeking recognition and rights, and on the cultural level of communities seeking ultimate meaning and faith, the diverse interpretations of human nature and destiny are shattering for many all sense of firm location in the world. To follow Herman Melville's image in *Moby Dick* of the world as ship in the midst of a voyage, pluralism means that differing maps are being given the passengers and divergent stories of where they have come from and what is their destination are being pressed upon them. It is in this way that pluralism has become a problem of the most profound sort for humanity.

Writes one observer: "Pluralism, the existence of various and contradictory approaches to life simultaneously, which can neither be uprooted nor overcome, absorbed or ignored, is the ideologically most threatening aspect of the modern world."[5] And specifically, when pluralism is so understood, it cannot fail to have a disquieting effect on human believing. Indeed, many regard pluralism as a mortal peril to all religious faith, to the entire theological enterprise, and in particular to Christianity.

What is the significance of pluralism for theology? Does religious faith have *no* meaning if it has multiple meanings? If we acknowledge that human beings believe in many gods, does it entail the dissolution of the notion of deity and the destruction of theology? I am persuaded that pluralism offers no such threat to theology, except to those varieties totally unable to accept or cope with change.

The implications of pluralism for theology depend first on the way religion is understood. If religion is taken to mean an unchanging core of divine truth, absolute in form and doctrine, then pluralism in any sense beyond the bare recognition of diversity can be seen only as dangerous error and a threat to the dogmas embodied in the one faith, whichever one that may be. In such a view, pluralism must be rejected as the latest guise of unbelief.

It is, of course, highly dubious that this understanding of religion has much to do with the actualities of human believing. Societal collectivities—economic, political, or ecclesiastical; conservative, liberal, or radical—may absolutize their teachings in the effort to gain or retain power. But human believing as rich compound of communal tradition and venturing faith can be discovered again and again, at different times and in diverse cultures, breaking through dogmatic barriers. The hunger of humans for the universal cannot be contained by pretenses of finality. Religious forms and formulations shape the life of a particular community in a given present; but the future relentlessly arrives, and change can no more be halted than King Canute could stop the waves of the ocean.

Without doubt, pluralism poses problems, indeed constitutes a threat, to those forms of religion and theology that seek to remain in an unchanging past, untouched by the responsibilities of the present or the insistent demands of the future. Pluralism, however, presents an intriguing challenge and unfolding possibilities for persons willing to wrestle with the meaning of change. Pluralism, in this perspective, is not so much a danger to religious faith, or to theology, as it is an opportunity to break out of the confines of the past and deal creatively with the revolutionary meaning of the future filled with human liberation.

The implications of pluralism for theology depend, in the second place, upon the way pluralism is understood. If pluralism in its cultural and religious dimensions is regarded as totally relativistic, then religious faith will be interpreted as social construction and human projection, useful or harmful fictions, depending on one's angle of vision. The multiple faiths that have guided various human communities in the past are exposed in this view as hopeful dreaming based on nothing firmer than collective illusion. All religions, in this view, must be regarded as fading pockets of opposition to relativistic realities.

There are, however, difficulties with drawing these implications from pluralism. An understanding of pluralism that slips into seeing itself as the single view bringing to an end all other views ceases to be pluralistic, in the same way that total relativism seems somehow contradictory because it applies the insight of relativity to all perspectives except its own. When pluralism and relativism are turned back upon themselves, they can scarcely be regarded as perils to the religious dimensions of human living. Instead they may provide opportunities for enrichment as faiths encounter one another. To be sure, pluralism presents problems, but it also opens new and exciting vistas for human believing.

The implications of pluralism for theology depend, in the third place, on the way theology is understood. If theology must by definition be restricted to a single ecclesiastical group or community of interpretation, then it can scarcely be expected to deal with pluralism. Plurality and the means for coping with it other than by total rejection are excluded by conceptual limitation. Theology understood as reflection upon the multiple convictions informing and shaping human action must confront, understand, and deal with the challenge of pluralism.

It is in no way surprising that theology in the conventional forms it has assumed in the academic traditions of Europe and North America is in turmoil as pluralism has made humanity vividly aware of multiple faiths and recalled the ancient view of life as an uncertain voyage on troubled and shifting seas. In conventional perspective, pluralism appears to confront theology with difficult if not impossible alternatives: either accept pluralism and abandon completely the affirmations of tradition concerning the reality of believed-in deity; or continue the old faith in its old forms with the old theological method which limits attention to a single community of faith. The first alternative attempts to assume an "objective" stance of noninvolvement by presuppositionless scholars and the generic study of religions "from a distance." How the scholar is to remain human and still attain a location stripped of perspective, assumptions, interests, and commitments has never been explained convincingly. The second alternative, the path still pursued by most academic theologians, utilizes a conceptual framework which systematically ignores or deals only peripherally with the diverse gods of human believing revealed by cultural pluralism.

Neither of these alternatives appears possible for theology as a global culture takes shape around us. It has become necessary, I am convinced, to reject the presuppositions that force such a choice upon us. This untenable situation derives from two primary sources. First, it comes from the ecclesiastical limits imposed upon, or passively accepted by, the conventional theology of North Atlantic academic centers. Second, the situation derives from the bifurcations of the Western intellectual tradition (i.e., accident/substance; existence/essence; appearance/being; subject/object;

phenomenal/noumenal; practical/theoretical; faith/ reality, etc.) within which most European and American religious thought has permitted itself to become imprisoned. In this Procrustean bed of artificially restricted vision and presupposed dichotomies, it is no longer possible to understand religious faith and deity in ways that permit theology to meet the challenge posed by the cultural configuration of pluralism.

Pluralism presents a continuing threat to theologies limited in their perspective to a single community of faith and operating in a bifurcated world. For such theologies, humans are divided into believers and unbelievers; their spheres of experience are split into the sacred and the secular; humans move from religious to nonreligious sectors of their lives; it is necessary to believe in some metaphysical deity out of the past or solemnly utter such nonsensical statements as, "God is dead."

Pluralism may perform a great service by liberating theology from these limitations, as theologians discover that it is no longer necessary to wear ecclesiastical and philosophical blinders. There are intriguing possibilities awaiting a theology bold enough to throw off bondage to these restrictions. Rather than peril, pluralism offers hope for a theology prepared to expand its scope beyond a single community of faith and include in its reflection the multiple and changing gods of human believing.

3. The Possibilities of Pluralism

The troubled scene of human culture resulting from the emergent pluralism that we see around us is not without parallel in the past. When faith in the pantheon of deities forming the sacred canopy of the Hellenic *polis* was shattered in the fourth century B.C., the Greek world suffered what Gilbert Murray has called a "failure of nerve." In the view of many, something of the same sort is occurring today, as the tribal enclaves of human meaning

appear to be dissolving in global pluralism. With the firm
sense of historical pattern given by sectarian faiths gone,
say these observers, there is no basis for a secure past, a
stable present, or a certain future.

While the difficulties are real, there is no convincing
evidence yet of massive cultural breakdown that could be
called a failure of nerve. Nor is it clear that we must resign
ourselves to cultivating the "nerve of failure." If we can
move beyond the self-pity that easily becomes despair
because we face the same problems of change and
disorientation similar to those faced by every generation,
we shall find resources for dealing with pluralism, even for
finding behind its threatening facade possibilities for faith
in the liberating God of biblical covenant.

To find such resources for theology, however, it is
necessary to turn in a direction most unusual for
theologians in America. I propose to draw on the thought
of an American theologian. This procedure is unusual
because theologians in the United States have tended to
ignore domestic thinkers and look to Europe for their
theological models. I call this phenomenon the colonial
mentality. Rather than follow this intellectual convention, let us look at the way H. Richard Niebuhr
formulates the task of theology. Because it emerges from
a context where pluralism has long been a prominent
factor, it is not surprising that Niebuhr's formulation
offers better guidance for dealing with this problem than
theologies originating in culturally and academically
insular settings of Europe.

Theology, Niebuhr reminds us, "is not simply an affair
of translating ancient ideas into modern language, but of
wrestling with ultimate problems as they arise in contemporary forms."[6] In this statement of the theological/ethical
task, Niebuhr reminds us of the continuing response to the
divine that every here-and-now requires. All too often,
theologians seek to escape the difficult issues of the present
by immersing themselves in the history of theology rather
than by doing theology. Or they describe the wrestling of
someone else in another time and place as a substitute for

their own dealing with ultimate issues faced by humans in the theologian's own time and place. We must learn from the past and from others, but such learning is *preparation* for theological reflection, not the doing of theology itself.

Niebuhr's statement deserves careful attention. In it he is pointing to several crucial aspects of what theology is and what it is not.

First, theology cannot perform its appropriate tasks in the here-and-now by repeating the formulas developed for a past era or for another continent. These concepts may have served the people and institutions well in their own time and place, but that does not mean that they fit the needs of our own situation. We can honor our past, acknowledge our debt to the heritage in which we have been nurtured, and learn from Europe or Asia without yielding to the illusion that respect requires literal imitation. On the contrary, we cannot be true to the daring spirit of Moses, of the prophets, of the early church, of Augustine, of Thomas Aquinas, of Martin Luther, of Dietrich Bonhoeffer, and of Martin Luther King, Jr., unless we are prepared to speak and act in innovative ways in order to respond, as each of them did in his own time, to new conditions in a changing world. Repeating ancient or alien ideas without first wrestling with the human condition in this time and place may be more a betrayal of our heritage than a continuation of it. We stand on the shoulders of those who have gone before us, not to repeat their words, but to strive to reach higher in our responses to the divine mystery as it breaks in upon us in ever-new ways.

Second, the wrestling with ultimate issues, which is required of theology in each new present, cannot be accomplished merely by linguistic transformations of concepts from their setting in other locations into contemporary speech forms. That is the task of translators, not of theologians. Such attempts at theology are inadequate because they are in fact veiled ways to hold on to the past rather than live in the present and also because they appear to assume that reality is static and that the dynamism of human believing derives from reinterpretation and the manipulation of language.

Third, the central point Niebuhr makes is that theology cannot do its proper work by evading the flow of events, by ignoring the changing context of history as we experience it in the present, or by resisting the continuing emergence of the future by taking refuge in theological formulations from the past. It is within and through the experienced world of natural-social-historical events, Niebuhr emphasizes, that we encounter that final sovereign reality which the Judeo-Christian tradition, as well as other communities of faith, understands as the divine mystery. Only as theologians wrestle with ultimate problems as they arise in contemporary form are they responding to the impingement upon human living of that "all-defining reality" (Wolfhart Pannenberg) that shapes the destiny of the whole. Only by such wrestling can Christian theologians be true in the present to the long heritage of contending with God, amid the onrushing events of human experience and relationships, that is depicted in the biblical Christian tradition. Though I can only speak from my own location in Christian faith, the same thing would seem also to be the case for Jewish and Moslem theologians, as they seek to be true to their particular traditions. It would appear to be the case also, with different language and emphasis, for other communities of faith. If this is so, then theologians of differing communities of interpretation and faith may learn from one another as they seek to identify and wrestle with reality as it appears in the present through issues emerging in the societal patterns and interaction of contemporary human living.

Fourth, pluralism can be seen both as an ultimate problem that theology must wrestle with today and also as a resource for understanding reality in increasingly comprehensive ways. In any event, pluralism enables theologians to be true to the past as well as to the present and future of their communities. Indeed, pluralism can become an agent for the liberation of theology. The liberation of theology today involves releasing theology from bondage to those formulations from the past that were once vital but now may be distant abstractions. Liberation does not mean rejecting the past. Instead it means being true to the tradition that has shaped us, which in every generation has produced persons willing to wrestle with the mystery of the divine. The liberation of theology means release of theology in the United States from bondage to Europe and of theology in the Third World from bondage to North Atlantic models.

Pluralism provides a way toward the responsible participation of theologians in the living community of their own faith, in relating to a widening spectrum of human communities as they continue the voyages of their forebears, and in joining the entire human community as it contends with the most challenging cultural configuration of our time. Because pluralism is among the most powerful ways ultimacy is pressing in upon human believing and acting today, the only peril it poses for theologians arises when they try to evade it by repeating formulas developed elsewhere and fail to seek its significance for contemporary faith.

In this perspective, the possibilities of pluralism for theology begin to emerge. Minimally, as a major problem in the emerging global culture, pluralism must be accepted as a condition of theological work. Beyond reluctant acceptance, however, pluralism points the way by means of which theology can again take up its tasks as a vital human enterprise. On the one hand, wrestling with pluralism opens possibilities for theology as a source of renewal within particular communities of religious faith. On the other hand, wrestling with pluralism can enable theology to respond once again to the contemporary actualities of human living, rather than repeating and analyzing old theological responses that served times long past.

I am convinced that, rather than being merely an unavoidable condition of scholarly work, pluralism offers significant possibilities for theology. As the meaning of pluralism emerges in its full religious and theological dimensions, it may return theology from the periphery to a central place in scholarly endeavor. It may be that pluralism will pose more difficult problems for a critical rationality, which remains imprisoned in the bifurcations of the Western intellectual tradition, than for a liberated, transformed theology.

As theology becomes informed by the possibilities of pluralism, it may develop patterns contributing to the renewal of religious communities. In 1962 the Graduate Theological Union was established in Berkeley. It was a pioneering effort in developing a theological faculty that brought Catholic, Protestant, and Jewish participants together in a common educational program; that utilized close relationships with other disciplines in the context of the University of California; and that immersed theological students in the multidisciplinary, multireligious diversity of the San Francisco-Berkeley area. Many in the churches feared that pluralism would undermine the faith of the seminarians—and perhaps also that of the professors as well.

With almost two decades in this ecumenical, inter-religious, pluralistic experiment gone by, it seems decisively clear that just the opposite has occurred. Close working contact with differing confessional, intellectual, and societal perspectives has had several discernible results.

First, it has led to *reinvigorated faith* on the part of the participants and the religious communities to which they are related. The plurality compels students and faculty to become more conscious of what they believe as individuals and as members of specific communities of interpretation. The dull atmosphere created by lack of significant difference and by the repetition of outmoded theological formulas and lifeless liturgies does more to prevent the development and deepening of faith than does an atmosphere of challenging diversity. One theological faculty, previously doing its work in an isolated location, had been on the verge of closing. Since its move to

Berkeley, and as a result of its participation in the Graduate Theological Union, it has become recognized as the strongest faculty of that religious group in the United States.

Second, the pluralistic context has encouraged the development of what might be called *creative borrowing* among the diverse religious traditions. Christians have been helped to rediscover and strengthen the Jewish elements in their heritage. With insight from the Hebraic sector of their past, Christians are less likely either to fade unthinkingly into the surrounding culture or to reject its contributions too easily. And of special importance, continuing contact with Judaism guards against the ever-present peril of Christianity based only on the New Testament. Amid the plurality, also, Protestants learn from Catholic spirituality and become conscious of the importance in a community of faith of what the Jesuits emphasize as religious formation. Catholics absorb into their own liturgical patterns the freer style of Protestant worship and begin to acquire "soul" from black Protestant congregations, singing more enthusiastically than the Methodists and developing more innovations than the Unitarians.

Third, in such a diverse context of theological discussion, it is no longer possible for the unquestioned verities of each confessional community to be repeated unchanged without challenge. Theologians must wrestle with faith as they have inherited it under new conditions and in relation to problems that are meaningful to persons of varied backgrounds. No better setting than a pluralistic one could be devised to jar complacent scholars, accustomed to working in separate confessional and disciplinary compartments, out of their conceptual frameworks and into what Niebuhr tells us is the continuing task of theologians, i.e., "wrestling with ultimate problems as they arise in contemporary forms."

Rather than undermining faith, pluralism, in the view from Berkeley, appears more as a means by which the deadly routines of traditional theology, liturgy, and practice may be infused with the vitality of renewed faith. The stories of our diverse faiths become alive again as we tell them to one another. And the life of one story is transmitted to other persons without necessarily destroying the power of believing within the communities of those who tell their stories or of those who hear.

At times, theology appears to be headed toward a stagnation of its own making. Such a situation is by no means inevitable. Pluralism, when seen, not as peril or as unavoidable necessity, but rather as opportunity, will enable theologians once again to recognize the multiple and changing gods of human believing and liberate theology to cope with the diverse and shifting character of societal and cultural experience. Once this recognition and this encounter have taken place, theology will discover itself undergoing a transformation that can lead to its renewal as a vital instrument for understanding global culture, as a means for analysis of human believing, and as a way for widening our religious consciousness in keeping with remembered promises of our own heritage and the emerging anticipations of diverse human histories.

IV.

REAPPEARANCE
OF THE GODS

Among the free shows offered on this bewitching planet, Berkeley ranks among the most intriguing and theologically instructive. A fascinating part of the human comedy is available there to anyone for the price of a stroll on one of the main streets. The playbill is a varied one, and the religious shows are especially interesting to me. Indeed, it was in Berkeley, as I walked along Telegraph Avenue and encountered eager believers hawking their faiths, that I first became vividly aware of the reappearance of the gods.

On one corner are the Hare Krishna dancers, their rustling bells and repetitive chant awakening anticipations of imminent epiphany. As I walk farther, the Asian music is drowned out by the strident voice of a fundamentalist preacher. He is haranguing a small audience of sun-drenched youth, their brown shoulders bare to the gods of nature; though his listeners are at most ten feet away, he is shouting at them that they are all dirty sinners in need of salvation.

Down the street, I encounter clear-eyed Jesus people darting about through the crowd distributing literature. Across Bancroft Way in Sproul Plaza, more rival gurus proclaim the gospel according to Marx, Mao, Sun Yung Moon, or Transcendental Meditation. If more evidence is needed of diverse deities, the variegated spiritual fare advertised on posters around Sather Gate would persuade me that the gods are definitely multiple and highly visible. With such a wealth of alternatives available, a person susceptible to conversion could change gods eight times in two blocks.

What appears to me with the intense color of Berkeley and San Francisco is occurring around the world. New York and Hamburg, London and Tokyo, experience the religious variety no less than California. A heightened awareness of human religiousness seems to be emerging everywhere. Old patterns of faith appear in new forms—as with the Jesus movement, the Western appropriation of Asian religions, and the revival in Iceland of worship of the old Norse god Thor. Even the conventional religion of the churches is undergoing renewal. And beyond the recovery of old patterns, there is also a seeking for new expressions of faith, crowding out gods that seem outworn and outgrown. Marxism and Maoism are perhaps to be counted also among the recent arrivals on the religious scene, reminding us that human believing has political dimensions and that political movements often acquire religious dimensions.

Does all this religiosity mean that dead gods have suddenly been resurrected? Not at all. On the contrary, deity—excluded for a time from the narrow range of vision permitted among positivists, considered beneath the notice of rationalists who saw an ever-improving humanity rising above "myth" and "superstition"—is again visible. So preoccupied had many students of religion become with observing and manipulating the empirical particulars of our world that the comprehensive meanings, which invest particulars with meaning and govern human action, had become submerged. The empiricists gave a limited kind of attention to religion. They counted members, studied trends in attendance, reported the amount of money donated, tabulated the rate of prayers per person, and kept track of the gate receipts—all the empirical data. They gave little attention to the empowering faiths that shaped human action and gave meaning to personal/communal existence.

Now we are again becoming conscious of varied ultimate commitments around us—to Mars and Aphrodite, to nation or church, to the gods of home and marketplace, to political and philosophical dogmas, to Buddha or to Jesus. Humanity has not suddenly become religious again after a time of non-religion; rather what had been ignored or invisible can again be seen, and so the gods are reappearing. We are becoming capable once more of discerning religious faith in the alternative patterns of loyalty and value informing the action and interaction of individuals, communities, and nations. It is not clear, however, that scholars in religious studies, and theologians in particular, are prepared to deal with these multiple and changing deities now coming into view.

1. Gods and Scholars

Pluralism in its theological dimensions is the meaning of the reappearance of the gods. One might expect theologians to be pleased, even overjoyed, at the widespread evidence of lively religious awareness. Instead of joy, or even interest, theologians have exhibited awkwardness and have come up with peculiar responses.

Eberhard Jüngel of the University of Tübingen, Germany, confesses to being overcome by great embarrassment in attempting to speak of God.[1] Variants of Jüngel's embarrassment underlie much of the theological turmoil of recent decades, from the controversies over demythologizing and secularization to the God-is-dead movement and the laboriously learned attempts to restore meaning to God-talk. The embarrassment of theologians has been very clear and very public.

While the scholars are embarrassed about God, human beings outside academic enclaves suffer no such difficulty. After a boxing match for the heavyweight championship, projected by the media into all parts of the world, one fighter gives thanks to God—the God of Islam; the other contestant gives equally emotional praise to God—the God of Christianity. Leaders of Israel, Egypt, and the United States seek peace in the Middle East in the names of their respective deities. Kings and queens are crowned with religious ceremonies invoking the divinity of their people. Presidents take solemn oaths to God when they enter office. Persons in parliaments and business attend prayer breakfasts. Thousands attend public rallies held to praise God, and millions attend worship services and listen to mass media programs where God is spoken for and about extensively. And, of course, in the bars and on street corners, the name of God is invoked on all occasions with no embarrassment at all. One might wish at times for greater care and more embarrassment among ordinary humans in speaking of God.

With so little diffidence exhibited in the world around by persons using God-talk, why are theologians embarrassed in speaking of God? One reason arises from a pervasive misunderstanding of the purpose and function of theology. Theologians often write as though it is their responsibility to discover or create language about God. This is, I am convinced, neither a necessary nor an appropriate task for theology. Human beings have been living and continue to live toward believed-in deities; and they speak of these gods a great deal. Theologians do not create religious believing, any more than grammarians create language. At most theologians can participate in the widespread human speaking of God, listen with care, and aid in articulating the continuing human wrestling with reality. Such wrestling is what religious believing is all about.

It is more accurate than not to say that humans cannot avoid speaking of God, though they may not always speak with care and precision. In this inescapability of speaking about God, humans are like the young man who discovered only when in the university that he had been speaking prose all his life. Given the pervasive religiousness of the human condition, it becomes clear that theologians do not originate religious living and speaking. These activities precede and surround theological reflection. Theologians may, however, perform important functions in illumining, ordering, and clarifying the varied, tangled scene of human believing.

Speaking of God is perhaps embarrassing, therefore, for theologians who misunderstand their task or their location, who may be under the impression that their speaking of God means speaking for God, or who regard their work as addressed only to previous theological literature rather than to the lively landscape of human wrestling with reality.

The basic reason for this condition of embarrassment, I am persuaded, is that Western theology remains imprisoned in the Constantinian paradigm, which determines the scope and methods of theological work. Theologians informed by this paradigm operate with notions of faith and religion that restrict their attention to institutional Christianity and to academic expressions of religious faith. All else is consigned to the "secular," that vague catch-all realm for whatever does not fit the restricted Constantinian mold. Thus, while the gods abound, conventional theology ignores them. For theologies limited to particular areas, the reappearance of the gods remains off-limits. Yet, outside their scholarly studies, theologians see and hear what is happening in society. The paradigm they are using is in profound dissonance with the lively religiosity of the world around them. And so they are embarrassed.

In this perspective, it becomes clear that the conceptual frame of much theology today renders the reappearing gods invisible. Thomas Luckmann makes a similar criticism of a kind of sociology of religion, the conceptual frame of which bears striking resemblance to that of a conventional theology. Luckmann charges that the work of this sociology has been limited to the institutional forms of Judaism and Christianity found in Western society.

> The main assumption—which also has the most important consequences for research and theory in the sociology of religion—consists in the identification of church and religion. . . . In the absence of a well-founded theory, secularization is typically regarded as a process of religious pathology to be measured by the shrinking reach of the churches. . . . The churches remain, in a manner of speaking, islands of religion (or irrationality) in a sea of secularism (or reason). . . . In any case the bulk of the recent sociology of religion is parish sociology.

This sociology has been capable only of charting the decline of institutional religion and its retreat from the center to the periphery of society in Europe and America. The forms of faith that are replacing traditional religion are therefore "invisible," excluded by an inadequate theoretical structure. Luckmann levels a serious accusation at the practitioners of this sociology of religion: they have failed to do their conceptual homework.[2] Indeed, one may wonder whether the findings of such a conventional sociology of religion tell us much at all about the changing scene of varied religious commitment in the modern world. Because it takes the organizational forms of the past as its conceptual yardsticks of religiousness, it may do nothing more than chart for our time the age-old tendency of prior organizational structures to be replaced or altered by succeeding generations.

Transferring Luckmann's critique of the sociology of religion to theology, we may say that theologians have not been doing their conceptual homework. The bulk of recent theology in Europe and North America has been ecclesiastical theology governed by the Constantinian paradigm. There has been an implicit identification of church with religion, and the further assumption that the task of theology is restricted to formulating the doctrines of a particular church or religious tradition. Because of the inadequate attention given to the notions of God, religion, and theology, the scope of what can be appropriately treated by theologians has become increasingly narrow. Anything beyond the faith of the theologian's own enclave, however conceived, has been left by most theologians to other disciplines.

For ecclesiastical theology, the world is divided conceptually into those who believe and those who do not. The former belong to the theologian's own religious group, however conceived, and the latter are all outsiders. The title of Michael Novak's book, *Belief and Unbelief,* suggests this oversimplified dichotomy. Gerhard Ebeling goes even further. He holds that the word "faith" needs no modifier to signify "Christian faith"; all else is "unfaith."[3] These positions have a certain circular coherence, but they are inadequate in dealing with the contemporary world of pluralistic believing. The dichotomy rests upon conceptual confusions with unhappy results for theology.

First, the varied patterns of human believing are obscured, or even rendered invisible. If we presuppose that persons outside our own community of faith are unbelievers, it impedes the inquiry into what these unbelievers believe and what significance their believing has for us. The realm outside our own enclave is lumped together as "secular," and pluralism is ignored.

Second, the standard of "faith" tends to become static, defined by some particular period of the past. The plural and changing character of the theologian's own tradition becomes difficult to perceive. Lutheran orthodoxy may become the standard of Christian truth for Lutherans. "Classical Christianity" can become the static measure of the authentic tradition for theologians retreating from the problems of pluralism. "Traditional belief " too easily becomes a means to reduce the complex past to a foil for contemporary argument. With such conceptual limitations, it becomes impossible for theology to deal with past changes, to chart the shifting character of human believing in the present, or to perceive the emergent global pluralism of our time and the reappearance of the gods.

Can theology break out of the confines of its Constantinian ecclesiastical past? Can theologians learn again, not simply to speak to their predecessors and to one another, but rather to address the actualities of human believing outside the churches as well as within them? Can new concepts and methods be found which will render the multiplicity of faith visible and usable in theology?

Late in his life, possibly because of pressure from critics, Karl Barth acknowledged the reappearance of the gods, an insight that had long hovered around the edges of his work. The task of theology, he wrote in this farewell series of lectures, is "to apprehend, understand, and speak of 'God.' " Rather than stopping there, however, he continued:

But many things can be meant by the word "God." For this reason, there are many kinds of theologies. There is no man who does not have his own god or gods as the object of his highest desire and trust, or as the basis of his deepest loyalty and commitment. . . . Every world view, even that disclosed in the Swiss and American national anthems, presupposes a divinity interpreted in one way or another and worshiped to some degree, whether wholeheartedly or superficially. There is no philosophy that is not to some extent also theology . . . an alternative object might be "nature," creativity, . . . "reason," progress, or even a redeeming nothingness. . . . Even such apparently "godless" ideologies are theologies.[4]

Such a statement is far too vague and amorphous to provide a stable conception of deity for a new theological paradigm. But it does point toward the plurality of human believing. In it Barth seems to be taking up again and extending the insights of his earlier book on Anselm, which marked a decisive turning point in his thought. Could it be that, at the close of his career, Barth would have liked to make still another beginning on his theology? Perhaps the reason he never completed the

Church Dogmatics is that the increasingly covenantal direction his thought took in Volumes III and IV would have required yet another beginning.

As Barth saw dimly, the task of theology is changing. The reappearance of the gods confronts theologians unavoidably with pluralism and requires concepts and methods that can deal with the multiplicity and change of human believing.

2. An Embarrassment of Riches

Coming from a darkened room into a sunny garden can be confusing and painful. The light strikes our eyes. The bright landscape is filled with shapes and colors that are overwhelmingly vivid to us but which we cannot see clearly. Then gradually, our eyes begin to accommodate to the new situation. We distinguish the large dark mass as trees and the patches of color as beds of flowers. Our eyes adjust further; our vision becomes more precise; we are able to bring memories of gardens we have seen before to bear on this scene around us. Now we recognize one tree as an oak, another as a birch, still another as an elm. The delicate shapes of the flowers become distinct. There are daisies, over there roses, at our feet a bed of peonies. What had been a jumble of impressions resolves itself into a garden, which we grasp in its wholeness and perceive in increasingly precise detail.

Something like this experience has been happening to theologians as contemporary society has been forcing them to leave the confines of sectarian and academic enclaves and come out into the culture of global pluralism. For the most part, they are unprepared conceptually to handle the new situation. Ernst Benz, in speaking of what he calls the new religions, describes the plight of theologians confronted with a changing reality: "But also Christian theology has tended to ignore the new religions, even to dispute the possibility of their development. For this theology, Christianity is the end and fulfillment of the history of religion; there can be no new religions." The world does not stand still for the convenience of ecclesiastical theology; as Benz observes, "The history of religion is not closed, but rather it is continuing."[5] The context of human believing is changing. The gods are reappearing. Coming out of the conceptual limitations of the past into the pluralistic present can be confusing and painful for theologians.

Whereas the restriction of ecclesiastical theology to a single religious enclave tended to make the gods of the "unbelievers" invisible, now with ecclesiastical blinders taken away a staggering, confusing variety of gods becomes visible. The bright landscape of religious believing dazzles us with its strange shapes, variegated hues, and delicate patterns. It is possible, as Ninian Smart suggests, to become "baffled by the variety"[6] of faiths. Or we may, in the words of Robert Bellah, become confused by the "plethora of religious phenomena in the contemporary scene."[7] With the limitations of the Constantinian paradigm gone, theologians will discover one embarrassment overcome but a new awkwardness looming, this time an embarrassment of religious riches.

Even in the ordinary, everyday level of human experiencing, the variety of human believing visible today is enough to confuse and baffle dedicated investigators. There may be few enough groups if we stick to the immediate neighborhood in which we live. But the number soon expands as our attention reaches farther to other nations with differing churches and many faiths. The missionary efforts of the various sects of Christianity have spread the confusion around the globe. Regional churches in Europe have become national denominations in the United States. Dutch Reformed groups are quite distinct from Swiss Reformed or Scottish Presbyterian groups. Scandinavian Lutherans belong to different churches, while Lutherans of German background are divided into several denominations. The Baptists are divided both by region and by European origin. Then these churches have carried out missionary

operations and established Swedish Lutheran congregations in Japan or Southern Baptist congregations in
northern China. Any understanding of religion must
clearly be able to deal with this variety.

Next, there is the plurality of so-called major world
religions—Judaism, Islam, Hinduism, Buddhism, Confucianism, Taoism, Shinto, Zoroastrianism, as well as
Christianity. And then there are also the animistic and
tribal cults of "primitive" groups around the world,
including the re-emergent Native American religions
and the worship of the old Norse gods. As communication and travel have reduced the size of the globe, many
of these faiths have not remained situated in the
countries of their origin but have, like Christianity,
spread to distant lands, become "world religions," and in
the process have changed. Hinduism in southern
California is different from what it is in India. Islam in
central Africa is not the same as in Arabia. The
differentiation that has accompanied the geographical
spread of Christianity has also occurred with other
religions. An understanding of religion must be able to
encompass this diversity.

But, of course, other major religions have remained no
more united than has Christianity, either in their original
settings or as they have spread. As Christianity is divided
into Roman Catholicism, Eastern Orthodoxy, and
Protestantism, with the further differentiation or fragmentation of each of these major sectors, so a similar
phenomenon is apparent in other religious traditions,
each having different streams with further divisions.
And, as with Christianity, these have spawned additional
variants as they have moved to new lands. Vedanta and
Hare Krishna are Hindu in background, but it may take
considerable sophistication in the study of religion to
recognize their common origin as one encounters them
in Hamburg or New York.

To the embarrassment of riches already before us must
be added also the "new" religions, some of which are
variations on old themes and some of which seem

genuinely new. Ernst Benz deals with a few of these
movements in the book mentioned above: the new
religions of Japan;[8] Cao-Dai in southeast Asia; the
Aurobindo Ashram; Baha'i; the Peyote Cult of North
American Indians; the Native American Church; the
Black Muslims in the United States; Ufology, the
interesting cult emerging around unidentified flying
objects; the Cargo Cult of New Guinea and Melanesia;
and the Messianistic Religions of Africa. But one might
also add the fascinating metaphysical cults of the United
States,[9] the Unification Church of Sun Yung Moon
spreading out from Korea,[10] and the Mormons, as well as
countless smaller groups that have sprung up around the
world.

To this wealth must also be added the "old" religions,
movements that have faded or disappeared but still must
be included in any comprehensive investigation of
human believing. In this group are the religions of
ancient Egypt, Babylonia, and Assyria; the mystery cults
of the Greco-Roman world; the pantheon of Olympus;
the religion of the Canaanite tribes; the faiths of
pre-Christian Europe; and heretical movements such as
Marcionism, Gnosticism, Manichaeism, Donatism, and
Albigensianism.

As we consider this variety, it becomes clear that any
notion of religion that can encompass this embarrassment of riches must be very general and flexible. Perhaps
Barth is correct that divinities presupposed in the Swiss
and American national anthems must also be included, as
well as movements centered upon nature, creativity,
reason, progress, or a redeeming nothingness. Naziism
and Marxism and Capitalism must be considered also for
inclusion as religious faiths and therefore appropriate
for theological investigation. To what extent, we must
ask, do all social and political movements have religious
dimensions? Is it possible that we must give attention also
to such diverse phenomena as communism and football?
However difficult the task, we must learn to deal with
religious diversity as it appears on the streets of Berkeley,

in changing societies around the world, and in the history of human believing.

3. A Question of Method

Once we admit the embarrassment of riches resulting from recognition of the reappearance of the gods, we can perceive how central is the question of theological method. How are we to deal with the variety and scope of human believing? How are notions of God and religion to be formulated so we may comprehend and give order to the multiple gods yet take account also of the intended realism of religious faith? How can we remain aware of our own location and perspective as believing humans while we attempt to understand the entire spectrum of believed-in deities?

To respond to these questions requires that long-neglected conceptual homework be done on behalf of theology and ethics. Issues of epistemology and cultural context must be considered in relation to religious faith. We must learn to include pluralism and liberation *within* theological methodology rather than viewing them as addenda. Understanding of change in relation to theology and human believing must be developed. In the most urgent and comprehensive sense, therefore, method is today the central issue for theology.

All the chapters that follow are my own attempt to wrestle with the problems of theological method. On the one hand, I am convinced that the Constantinian paradigm governing Western theology since the fourth century is being shattered. On the other hand, it is equally clear to me that a covenantal or federal paradigm offers a method for theology and ethics in continuity with the biblical Christian heritage, yet capable of coping with the pluralism and liberation of the emerging global culture. Exploring the transformation of theology from a Constantinian to a federal model provides the arena for dealing with methodological issues.

WHEN GODS CHANGE

The first step in reconceiving the task and method of theology will be to examine the light that pluralism throws on human location and perspective. Once we understand the mystery of location as the condition of our humanity, we are tempted neither to adopt the arrogance of the imperial mood in theology nor to capitulate to the claims of epistemological relativism.

The second step involves exploring the impact of cultural change upon contemporary theology, how the relation between change and human believing can be reconceived, and what it means to speak of theological transformation. In the process, we shall try to understand the starting point of theological reflection within the covenantal wholeness of human experiencing rather than in the bifurcated world of the Western intellectual tradition.

In the third step of reconceiving our theological method, I shall elaborate a federal paradigm. On the one hand, this takes us into a covenantal epistemology, with its historical and communal dimensions of human knowing. On the other hand, it takes us into the reconceptualization of the notions of religion and God, which we have described as too limited within the Constantinian paradigm. And at the heart of the federal paradigm is liberation, the principle through which we can understand the meaning of salvation and the dynamics of history.

My view that theology is undergoing major change and my proposal for a transformed method place me at odds with most conventional forms of theology as well as disclose my unhappiness with the theological fads of recent years. Conventional theology remains trapped in the outmoded patterns of the past. The fads, on the other hand, represent eccentric responses to the crisis of change that the Constantinian paradigm is going through, yet they fail to escape its difficulties.

Edinburgh theologian Thomas F. Torrance provides an example of a carefully developed theology that in style and method is heavily dependent upon what I am calling the Constantinian paradigm. Traces of the old covenant theology persist in this Scottish thinker as he refers to "the *faithfulness* of God" and adds, "We still believe that God is reliable and faithful, and that form and order belong to the fabric of the universe."[11] But his theology is for the most part narrowly ecclesiastical.

Torrance interprets Barth to mean that the proper task of theology is "to think through the whole of theological knowledge in such a way that it might be consistently faithful to the concrete act of God in Jesus Christ from which it actually takes its rise in the Church." Faith appears to be turned into knowledge by Torrance: "In scientific theology we begin with the actual knowledge of God, and seek to test and clarify this knowledge by inquiring carefully into the relation between our knowing of God and God Himself in His being and nature." This knowledge provides Torrance with a transcendent perspective, an ontological peak, from which to speak in the imperial mood: "Divine actuality and historical facticity are thus inseparably united in the ground of our knowledge and are not to be torn apart in our continuing inquiry into the face of Jesus Christ." He rejects religion as leading to idolatry: "Whenever religion is substituted in the place of God, the fact that in religion we are concerned with the behaviour of *religious people,* sooner or later means the substitution of humanity in place of religion—the point at which our 'secularizing' philosophies of religion appear to have arrived." But he has no such fears when "theological science must step in to help men refer their thoughts properly beyond themselves to God."[12] Theology of this kind exhibits continuing currents of Constantinianism in contemporary theology.

Bernard Lonergan, who also has done careful work on theological method, represents some limited shifting away from the traditional paradigm. Method for Lonergan is not static but "a normative pattern of recurrent and related operations yielding cumulative and progressive results."[13] He explicitly expresses dissatisfaction with scholasticism:

Scholastic theology was a monumental achievement. . . . Yet today by and large it is abandoned. . . . The scholastic aim of reconciling all the elements in its Christian inheritance had one grave defect. It was content with a logically and metaphysically satisfying reconciliation. It did not realize how much of the multiplicity in the inheritance constituted not a logical or metaphysical problem but basically a historical problem."[14]

Lonergan carefully includes the historical approach in his theological methodology and does not lapse into the imperial mood. He writes, "Because a theology is the product not simply of a religion but of a religion within a given cultural context, theological revisions may have their origin, not primarily in theological but rather in cultural developments." But the rational and philosophical style remains dominant. In similar fashion, Lonergan perceives the problem of pluralism, yet sees a rational solution to it: "But behind this multiplicity there is a basic unity that comes to light in the exercise of transcendental method." And further, theological pluralism for Lonergan is primarily the diverse expressions of Christianity, and "What builds the bridges between the many expressions of the faith is a methodical theology."[15] It is not surprising, therefore, to discover a similar limitation in Lonergan's student, David Tracy. Tracy professes to be writing a book dealing with pluralism and tells us at the beginning: "That the present situation in theology is one of an ever-increasing pluralism is by now a truism."[16] He is referring, however, only to the diversity of Christian theology. Global pluralism and its significance for theology is not yet a truism for him, nor has it arrived within his horizon. Lonergan and Tracy illustrate theology that is indeed changing, but they still remain in many respects tied to the Constantinian paradigm.

John Cobb in *Christ in a Pluralistic Age* confronts directly the global variety of great traditions and chooses Buddhism "as a particularly important example of the kind of tradition in the face of which Christian theology should reconceive Christ." From the perspective of a process theology dependent upon Alfred North Whitehead's philosophy, Cobb sees creative possibilities for Christian thought in the critical acceptance of pluralism. Christ must be reconceived as creative transformation in all human experience and not bound to the historical Jesus or to any past doctrine. "When Christ is known as this power of creative transformation and when faith is wholeheartedly directed to him, pluralism can be inwardly appropriated without relativism." He perceives also the liberating potential of the position he envisions, for "the Christian consciousness must be freed from its fear that to move forward in the acceptance of the secular and pluralistic world threatens its faithfulness to Christ."[17] More than most theologians, Cobb recognizes the dimensions of pluralism, and he sees the need for change in theology. When we understand the heavy reliance of Cobb's theology on process metaphysics, however, we realize that basic elements of the Constantinian paradigm remain.

As we see clearly from these examples, theological method is at the heart of diverse theological problems today. The work of Lonergan, Tracy, and Cobb demonstrates that significant changes are taking place. But it is also clear that we must go even further in reconceptualizing theological notions and transforming theological method.

This is an ambitious undertaking. Specialists in one or another of the fields I touch may be dissatisfied with the detail and precision of the discussion. Even so, I hope to evoke multidirectional interaction among the variety of disciplines and perspectives needed to deal with the fascinating problems of theology in the global culture. Perhaps our investigation will also contribute to overcoming the superficiality of over-specialization in regard to human believing, in the study of which learned persons of limited vision make no small errors on the way toward grand fallacies.

V.

THE MYSTERY
OF LOCATION

The configuration of pluralism can be seen vividly today in the mingling of diverse meanings, the meeting of different ethnic groups, and the competition of divergent cultural interpretations in the emerging global culture. In theological perspective, pluralism directs our attention to the varied and changing gods of human believing as deity once again becomes visible. There is another aspect of pluralism, an aspect with important implications for theological method: pluralism makes us aware of human location.

In its most immediate and obvious sense, pluralism discloses humanity in midpassage, between a whence and a whither. Pluralism thrusts upon us the insight that we are on a voyage with no consensus among the passengers as to origin or destination, the correct charts to use for orientation, the proper direction of travel, or the meaning of the journey. The diversity of interpretations held by societal groups other than our own strikes us first in our pluralistic world. Turned back upon our own interpretation of ourselves and our way of life, however, pluralism raises the issue of our own perspective and location. Where are we? By what means do we understand who we are and where we are? And how do we determine the direction to take from where we believe ourselves to be?

Pluralism, as it has impinged upon human conscious-ness, has shattered the notion of fixed location for ordinary humans in much the same way that historical consciousness and relativism had earlier dispelled the sense of firm ground to stand on for Western intellec-tuals. But it has done even more. Pluralism has relentlessly pressed upon us the relation of location and perspective. And perspective as rooted in a particular location provides understanding of self, others, and deity. But location for humans is within communities with traditions and historical interpretations. Location, therefore, becomes a central issue for theological method, an issue with far-reaching implications. For location, as disclosed by pluralism viewed in theological perspective, is not only varied and uncertain for humans. Human location is also a mystery. Let me explore this mystery in terms of my own background of growing up in the southern part of the United States.

When I was very young, between the magical ages of five and ten, the world was for me a wondrous, spacious, and varied place. In a single afternoon, once the unreality of school with its boring little lessons was left behind, I could choose among a rich diversity of glowing realities to explore.

To the east of my home, behind a neighbor's house, was a wild and private jungle. There my friends and I entered a covenanted world where Tarzan, his animals, and his friends, the pygmies, lived. We would swing through the branches or slip silently through the bushes to rescue captured wanderers and utter triumphant jungle yells. Our neighbor, an older business man, would sometimes drive us away with a scowl. But his sister, when he was not at home, would feed us cookies and lemonade on the back porch.

To the north of my home lived an ill-tempered witch,

who we believed ate children if she could catch them. We risked our lives exploring the subterranean cavern beneath her castle. If she discovered us, she would pursue us, shout imprecations, and even threaten to complain to our parents.

To the south lay a great plain covered with broomstraw and small trees. Several limbs, stuck into the ground in a circle, tied together at the top, and woven around with broomstraw, made an excellent tepee for our tribe of Indians. We roamed the plain seeking game, scalping unwary settlers, and performing intricate dances in our villages.

If the weather was cold or rainy, my bookshelf offered other worlds. The land of Oz always awaited me. The Hardy boys and Tom Swift invited me to join their adventures. James Fenimore Cooper would transport me into early America. Walter Scott would take me to Europe. When I tired of reading, there was a palace hidden deep beneath my home where I ruled a vast realm as absolute potentate, with subjects ever eager to do my bidding and untold wealth at my disposal.

The afternoon over, I joined my family for supper. And at the table, I glimpsed the worlds inhabited by my parents, brothers, and sister. Usually with laughter and light, sometimes with sparks and fire, and always with warmth and dancing illumination, I learned of realms beyond the ones I already inhabited, worlds with wider horizons than my most extravagant dreams, waiting to be explored. I lived at the intersection of manifold realities, some partly known, others reflected in the experience of others.

But it was not all expanding magnificence. There was also an ugly and puzzling contradiction. In the social reality of the southern states, side by side, were the comfortable world of the white middle class and the constricted world of oppressed blacks. I grew up in this segregated society. But I also went to a Christian church where I was inducted into another reality in which I learned to sing:

> Jesus loves the little children, all the children of the world;
> red and yellow, black and white, they are precious in his
>   sight.
> Jesus loves the little children of the world.

Few more painful things have happened to me in my life than those that occurred as I began to contrast the reality of Christian justice and love with the practices of southern society. My multiple worlds grated against one another and threatened to tear me apart. I had to choose which reality I would follow, which location I would choose as my own. The turmoil and the mystery of human location swept over me. My choice took me into Christian ministry and into movements for human rights, but it also alienated me from many sectors of the society into which I had been born. To choose among the alternative locations offered me meant at last choosing an identity, choosing a community of interpretation, affirming a faith, and glimpsing the moving face of deity.

1. Dimensions of Human Location

Alfred North Whitehead is undoubtedly correct in saying that nothing has the property of simple location. Clearly this is the case with reference to human experience. From our earliest years, we encounter diverse worlds that expand and multiply as our experience broadens. We exist in history as a fish exists in water. It is the context and medium of our developing awareness. And so, as humans, we occupy locations that are complex, that are changing, that in their tangled wholeness comprise a vivid, variegated mystery.

In pursuit of understanding, I may ask a grandly ontological question, such as, "Why is there something rather than nothing?" But the grammar, the connotations, and the horizon of possible meanings of the question have been shaped by my socio-historical context long prior to the time when I reached a high enough level of sophistication to be interested in posing it. So it is also with all our theological and philosophical speaking. What appears clear, even obvious, to us fades, when we pursue it carefully, into the mystery of human location.

On a level nearer to ordinary experiencing, I may ask: "Why was I born in Western society, in the United States, in North Carolina, in a small town, the youngest of six children?" How can such a question be answered? The *why* questions, whether posed in simple bewilderment or with intellectual pretentiousness, apparently have no final answers, or indeed any answers at all that are not finally themselves enigmas.

But we may also ask the *where* questions. "Where was I born?" "Where do I live now?" "Where is my home?" These questions are even more deceptive than why questions because they may appear to have unambiguous answers. The naming of a place in answer to these questions, the naming of a "simple" location, serves only to conceal the complexity of human location.

To speak with understanding of *where* we are requires recognition that our location is not in empty space defined by geometrical coordinates or geographical nomenclature. Humans live in community, in relationship, in time and history. We live in diverse realms of memory, of imagination, and of hope, into which we have been inducted by the interaction and rites of the communities in which we are born and into which we emerge with developing awareness. As we look around us and examine our location, we can distinguish dimensions or components. These elements are not separable from one another but belong together in a living wholeness of human experiencing. This wholeness has clarity and coherence at the center of our consciousness but merges into vaguer patterns and at last into mystery on the edges of awareness.

THE MYSTERY OF LOCATION

What are some of the dimensions of human location that are distinct enough to identify?

1. *The space of human location is inhabited space.* The abstract space of the geometer's calculations is unknown in human experiencing, except when we deliberately focus on something we have created by stipulation or mathematical rule in order to deal with certain problems. Location as inhabited is filled with and constituted by human relations that surround us, permeate our sense of selfhood, and intrude into our most abstract speculations, even into times when we are most alone. Human action and interaction encompass us at home and on the job, in community and church congregation, in economic and political affairs, in national and international relations. Encounter with other humans ranges from caress of love to threat of violence, from those whom we know and love personally to film stars and political figures whose activities we follow avidly in the mass media, and from individual conversations to interaction in large groups as at a football game, in a national election, or in the timely timelessness of a worship service. We inhabit space that is inhabited by others.

2. Because it is inhabited, *human location has an atmosphere of wariness and watchfulness.* We do not always know what actions to expect or what reactions may come in return to our own actions. There are known and unknown threats to our physical safety, to our sense of personal worth and dignity, to our purposes and loyalties, that require us to surround ourselves with various devices for defense. There are hopes and beliefs and loves that call forth our energies, draw us outside our defenses, and entice us to take risks. The terrain requires caution, but it does not permit us to withdraw into security or isolation.

3. *Human location is timeful,* filled with a sense of past and future, time passing, moving toward an end, opportunities missed, happiness enjoyed, suffering endured. Happening, action, and change mark the

movement from one present to another. And each present is itself filled with time, brimming over with remembrance and reaching out with anticipation to embrace the future. The present is not so much a knife-edge as the crowded moving focus of many forces, some with a high valence for us, others of little importance. Each present can scarcely contain the varied memories and hopes, the hurts and fears, the obligations and loyalties, the overt and covert purposes that shape our action and comprise our awareness of time. The clock ticks, and the hands move; but the time of human location is not measured in meters or in minutes but rather in the measures of faithfulness and unfaithfulness.

4. *Human location means particularity.* All those elements by means of which we locate ourselves—community and relations; wariness and steady watchfulness; remembered past and anticipated future co-present in a timeful now with loves and fears—are not before us as general categories to be considered dispassionately at a distance but are vivid particulars permeating ourselves and our worlds. The specific particulars are different events even for siblings in the same family. The specifics differ even more for persons in different communities and more still for those in widely different cultures. Regardless of the differences that we become aware of quite early, each of us lives amid particular circumstances that add up to particularity of location, particularity that distinguishes us from others and also binds us to all our human companions. Quite early, we become aware of the particularity and of the plurality of human location. As our experience expands, the variety of both broadens. Yet even in the plurality of particular locations, continuity and relation persist. In spite of distance and difference, we can empathize with persons starving on another continent; we are able in part to understand and dwell in a dialogue of Plato from ancient Greece; we can find ourselves being awakened to faith in a Hebrew God by accounts of exodus and deliverance two millenia old or

called to new life by stories of Jesus suffering on a cross from two thousand years ago. Particularity, plurality, and continuity are inseparably interwoven in human location.

5. *Human location means history.* We may make the mistake of assuming that human location is adequately described when we have assembled and labeled its major components. Not at all! Understanding as much as we can of this mystery requires more than identifying and arranging the conceptual furniture. That would be constructing the scenery and placing the props on the stage and thinking we have all that is needed for a play. Or collecting artifacts and rebuilding buildings and thinking we have recaptured a society. A play requires plot as well as props. Society involves meanings, patterns, and values that actual humans believe in and live toward; that is, a culture. Inhabited space, filled with timeful particulars, does not become human location until we have included the story that binds these together into lived meaning. The "place" where we dwell as humans has relations and events woven together into a history. Indeed it is the history as the story of our lives that invests all the other parts with significance. The story describes our location and fills that space with moral valence and directive. Human location as history is inescapably religious and therefore susceptible to theological and ethical analysis.

6. *Location for humans also means involvement.* Not only is location inhabited and particular, and filled with wariness, time, and pattern; it is also a locus of identity, where selfhood is received and expressed. Beyond merely inhabiting location, we as humans dwell in it with the involvement of our whole selves. We believe in this location; we are committed to it.

Perhaps the way that we become involved in a play or novel can aid in understanding the involvement of human location. We pick up a book, for example, an adventure story. Within its covers we encounter at first only pages filled with words arranged into sentences, paragraphs, and chapters. The book is paper covered with ink in recognizable patterns. Then we begin to read. We discover soon the setting of the story. We are introduced to the characters and learn gradually about their dreams, schemes, and fears. Our interest increases as we accompany them through times of tension and danger. The story draws us into its world. We become involved with these people, their interaction, their location. We come to dwell in the world of the novel with such intensity that the place of our own everyday existence fades into the background. Our time merges into the time of the story. So intently are we listening to the sounds in the story that we fail to hear the doorbell ring. We are sitting in a chair in our own living room, but that place and this story have become springboards sending our imagination into the places depicted in the novel. The knife with which one character kills another takes on more reality than the one resting safely in our kitchen drawer. Through the writer's art and our own imaginative involvement, the paper and ink, the paragraphs and chapters, have been transformed into human location.

With even greater intensity, seriousness, and wholeness, human location means involvement of the participants in the story of their lives and commitment to it. This commitment does not necessarily mean liking all of one's world. It means rather knowing that one's identity and existence as a person derive from and are invested in this world. This involvement does not develop slowly, as when we pick up a novel. In the story of our lives, involvement is a given from beginning to end. Only by suicide can persons even attempt to escape involvement in the location given them with their existence.

Though our lives are made up of varied components, distinguishable in their particularity, it is our dwelling in the meaning of their interrelated wholeness that transforms time and place into human location. The meaning of the whole, invested with significance of identity and involvement, provides the decisively human element of location.

7. Finally, *human location means reality.* Indeed, identity and involvement point inescapably toward communally held ideas of reality, as do language and imagination.

Humans do not live toward illusion but toward believed-in reality. We speak of illusions, but this is possible only from the perspective of a reality which excludes other views as unreal. In the same way, we speak of false religions and false gods only from the perspective of what we believe in as true religion and true deity. Doubts derive not primarily from skepticism but secondarily from perspectives that cause us to raise questions. So-called critical rationalism, valuable as it may be, does not exercise its power outside a frame of presupposed criteria and believed-in reality.

Human locations are actuality for those who dwell in them. Each location involves its in-dwellers in a believed-in reality, in a perspective grounded in the sense of final sovereignty and power, within which events take place and by which the wholeness of location and its parts are defined. This reality provides the criteria for what is true and what is false, the source of legitimation of societal forms and the validation for patterns of moral action.

For this reason, an understanding of myth or religion that takes a distant, patronizing view of them fails to penetrate to their inner meaning. A myth comes into being and exists because some community once did or still does believe in it as depicting the sovereign reality of that community's human location. Those who define myth as illusion overlook the mythic dimensions of the believed-in reality of their own location. And those who attempt to demythologize forget that they too occupy human location.

Even as we name these dimensions of human location, however, we recognize that other ways could be used to organize and describe the wholeness of our experience. Other cultural locations might require different divisions and nomenclature. From my own Western perspective, varied terms are used to describe similar experienced realities. Most obviously, we could speak of selves emerging and acquiring self-understanding in community and of that community being given pattern and identity by its historical consciousness and by the believed-in deity that shapes its action. This terminology is especially helpful as we explore the meaning of human location for theological method.

To distinguish the elements of human location, however, in whatever language we use, does not exhaust the complexity or eliminate the mystery. We may see our environs better. We may understand in part the changes and continuities of particular perspectives. We may comprehend the variety of human histories, but we are not thereby lifted to an absolute view of all reality. Our location remains human.

2. Selves in Community

"We are all children of our landscape," writes Lawrence Durrell. Or, to say the same thing in terms we have been using, self-awareness begins with the acknowledgment of our human location. And that recognition has far-reaching implications for theological method. As we explore these implications, the communal context of experience and self-awareness, of language and what we call knowledge, and of human believing emerges. From there, it is not far to a better understanding of what we mean when we speak of history and of God.

To discover the ways of human worlds, to understand in part the mystery of human location, is to glimpse selfhood as the elusive center of experience. In our ordinary understanding a self is so frequently depicted as an isolated, individualistic billiard ball of substance that the rich relationality of experienced selfhood has been obscured for many. Selves do not arise in isolation.

THE MYSTERY OF LOCATION

Individuals are not known and do not develop awareness of themselves apart from the interactive context of human community. Individuality in its experienced intensity cannot be reduced to communal relations. But neither can the textured awareness of our individuality be disentangled from its relational fabric and be regarded as a thing or an essence apart from community. To understand better this inseparable interrelationality of self and community, let us reflect on what we know about how selves come into being.

Just as the experience of humanity generally is one of being in midpassage, so also emerging into self-awareness as individuals is discovering that we are joining a process already under way before we arrive. There are people around us already relating to one another and to us. We enter a family that existed prior to our awareness. We belong to a community that extends beyond the family and antedates it. Both family and wider community exist in a world with unknown bounds in time and space. But this extended awareness dawns on us only gradually.

We can, on one hand, look back and reflect on the emergence of our own selfhood only from a later standpoint already shaped by our community of interpretation. Those who formed this community when we arrived on the scene have in their interaction with us taught us how to relate, given us a language with which to communicate, and passed on to us the perspective of the community. On the other hand, we may seek to understand how selves come into being by observing what happens with later arrivals in our own community or studying the observations made of the young by others, in our own or in other communities. This latter way has more possibility of being checked and corrected by others, but it lacks the sharp sense of inner awareness that is central to selfhood. Both ways can be helpful, but both occur, we should remember, within a context of reflection that is highly developed and already shaped by a community of interpretation, not from an immediate view of selfhood that has no presuppositions or prior formation by one or another community. This circumstance need not dampen the eagerness or diminish the importance of our seeking. But remembering it continually may make us more modest in our claims about the results that we achieve. We seek to understand our human location from within that human location.

Human experiencing begins apparently before we achieve reflective consciousness. By combining our own memories with studies observing the development of infants, we can infer that consciousness and the sense of selfhood are shaped by a context existing before the developing self discovers it. In spite of the difficulties we encounter as we attempt to penetrate back into this process of development, the reflective awareness of present location certainly offers no grounds for a solipsistic interpretation of our existence. At no point do we have self-awareness apart from awareness of a context of other selves, communal relations, and a world. Indeed, our sense of wariness and precariousness in existence and the anticipation of death both as end and as threat strongly suggest the dependence of selfhood on surroundings rather than of surroundings on self. Only a sophisticated consciousness dealing with abstractions far distant from ordinary experience could arrive at the grand philosophy of subjective idealism. Self and communal surroundings are inescapably compresent for us in our developed experiencing, and the communal, biological, and physical surroundings appear to have a temporal priority.

As we trace human awareness back toward its emergence, we discover that a highly imaginative and persuasive case can be made for the undifferentiated wholeness of experience both in so-called primitive societies and in the "primitive" awareness of infants. Studies of primitive peoples conclude that their consciousness exhibits wholeness, without the multiple bifurcations in the European intellectual tradition that underlie much of our philosophy and theology. In marked contrast to this Western nexus of presuppositions, a sharp split between self and surroundings, between inner and outer, between subject and object, does not appear to exist in primitive human experience.[1] In similar fashion, very young children seem unaware of these dichotomies in their world until communities of interpretation that presuppose them have carefully trained the young to accept the split world of tradition.[2]

Undoubtedly, the distinction between inner and outer may come to have meaning for us as we increase the differentiated awareness of our experiencing from the "blooming, buzzing confusion" of the infant's earliest world (William James) to the highly developed knowledge of physics and chemistry, engineering and management, biology and anthropology, social science and the humanities, theology and art. Differentiation and bifurcations have been important in learning to manipulate, control, and alter our environment. Yet, even as we go through the series of human cultural capabilities from the physical sciences to life sciences and social skills and then on to art, we recognize increasingly the importance of understanding not only in pieces but also in wholes. Indeed, on what basis can we ascribe to a differentiated part or a bifurcated sector of experience greater reality or more inclusiveness than the wholeness within which each occurs? How is it possible to assign ontological or epistemological priority to one side or another of a presupposed bifurcation when both sides have meaning only together and only as inseparable parts of an experienced whole? Inner experience is a function of a totality that includes the outer. Outer experience has no significance for us apart from a perspective that includes the inner. Where or when do we encounter subject apart from a context of objects, or an object apart from a perceiving subject? Neither exists in our experience split off from the comprehensive entity of wholeness.[3]

We may be grateful to Martin Heidegger in *Sein und*

Zeit for reversing the practice of assigning priority to the factual, objective world opened to Western humanity by Newtonian physics. He showed with brilliant and delicate analysis how objects are extensions of self-awareness toward abstraction. Yet why should we accept the presupposition of a bifurcated world that compels us to choose between Newton with his varied followers and Heidegger with the distinguished galaxy of phenomenologists and existentialists who are in diverse degrees his companions in this great inversion of ontological priority? Humans cannot divest themselves of location in being and time in order to achieve a "direct," extra-human view of a presupposed "objective" reality. But, on the other hand, we cannot place our surroundings and our communal relations on a subordinate level and deal with reality as isolated existing selves alone in the mountains filling blank pieces of paper with ultimate truth. The wholeness of our fundamental experiences seems to be an interpenetrative unity that we later differentiate, for various purposes, into inner and outer.

In subsequent sections (chapters 8 and 9), we shall have occasion to contrast further the wholeness of human experiencing with the dichotomies of the European intellectual tradition. At the moment, we are exploring the mystery of human location, tracing the highly differentiated quality of developed awareness back toward a more primal wholeness.

No location for humans, even a primitive one, can be regarded as simple. But it seems clear that the context out of which selfhood emerges and into which selfhood merges is an already-existing location of selves interacting with one another in communal surroundings.

From this perspective, we may say that we emerge into awareness as selves within relationships. John Macmurray writes: "Against the assumption that the Self is an isolated individual, I have set the view that the Self is a *person,* and that personal existence is *constituted* by the relation of persons."[4] Selfhood exists, comes into awareness, and is shaped in its awareness within community. But communities must not be thought of as some ontological ultimate. Communities are made up of interacting selves in a surrounding environment. It seems impossible to distinguish a community as an entity apart from the individuals comprising it or to distinguish individual selfhood in isolation from the interacting, interpenetrating selves of communal relations.

Our awareness of selfhood develops in a social context, and our awareness of society develops in a context of selves. It is more than a matter of self awaking to selfhood and subsequently discovering its existence in a particular location and relations. The self is social in its constitution and character. As each of us comes to awareness within a context of interacting selves, it is in the mirror of the responses of others to us that we come to regard ourselves, achieve self-awareness with firm identity, and attain understanding of who this self is that learns to say *I* and is able to respond when addressed. This development of the social self begins in the primary communities of our infancy and childhood and continues as the communities of our interaction expand and become diverse. Writes George Herbert Mead:

The self, as that which can be an object to itself, is essentially a social structure, and it arises in social experience. After a self has arisen, it in a certain sense provides for itself its social experiences, and so we can conceive of an absolutely solitary self. But it is impossible to conceive of a self arising outside of social experience.[5]

The context in which self-awareness emerges is not only relational and social; it is also tactile. The relationship in the earliest community for the human infant takes place primarily by means of touch. The experiencing of the infant develops and is given pattern by the communication provided in being touched and fondled and in the infant's touching and handling. Without continuing tactile communication and action, the infant organism will not grow nor the world of the infant develop. Touching, stimulation, and the action of responding are not incidental but essential to human growth. Margaret Ribble, reporting on investigations of the mysterious infant ailment called marasmus, says that the infant that is not touched and fondled will waste away and that the action of touching and sucking on the part of the infant is necessary for the development of the cerebral cortex.[6] In tactile interaction, the experiencing self begins to emerge, and the self's potential for dwelling in an expanding world is nurtured.

This context of human interaction also conveys to the developing self what we come to call meaning. In its earliest and most elemental sense, meaning is conveyed on an inarticulate level. Contact with mother, father, siblings, and others has great meaning for an infant, as surely as language will at a more developed stage. Patterns of touching, feeding, and sleeping, patterns of being with persons and being alone, and patterns of sound and light take shape, conveying meaning in the relations and interactions. These earliest meanings are not superseded by later ones but rather become the context in which subsequent meaning is articulated and interpreted. Experiencing emerges, therefore, not so much as differentiated parts, but rather as a field of valency within which new occurrences are located and modify the pattern of the whole. The wholeness of experiencing, as its valencies are shaped by dominant relationships and memories, continues to inform our interpretation and action in each new present. Sometimes the power of the past is so great as to distort present realities. Rollo May provides a striking illustration:

It is one thing to discuss the hypothesis of aggression as resulting from frustration, but quite another to see the tenseness of a patient, his eyes flashing in anger or hatred, his posture clenched into paralysis, and to hear his half-stifled gasps of pain from reliving the time a score of years ago when his father whipped him because, through no fault of his own, his bicycle was stolen—an event giving rise to a hatred which for that moment encompasses every parental figure in his whole world, including me in the room with him. Such data are empirical in the deepest meaning of the term.[7]

Such instances depict vividly how the present does not supersede the past but comes under its power.

The context of meaning within which our earliest memories are set is cultural. It is meaning that belongs to the community before we arrive on the scene. We receive and respond to patterns existing before our appearance. Gradually we are inducted into this community of interpretation, take our place within its relationships and interactions, and participate in revising its interpretations and passing them to subsequent arrivals.

The meaning already present is better understood not so much as propositions as valencies, commitments, love and loathing, warmth and tension. These feelings felt as realities shape the action and interaction within our community, and as we are inducted into these meanings they also shape our actions. The loyalties of the community become our loyalties, its commitments ours, its beliefs ours. These communities into which we arrive are filled with covenants already made in which we are called to join. Covenants have been made for us, to us, around us, with promises already implied that we are asked to receive and affirm, with memories and anticipations that we are expected to make our own. The tradition of family, the hopes of parents, the call to patriotism, confront us in our community. We affirm them and gain the confidence of belonging. Or we question and refuse to give our whole-hearted loyalty and feel uneasy, outside the mainstream, and inadequate. Meaning in this sense is not about differentiated parts of our world but rather is a field of force, an integrated wholeness of covenantal relations.

This field of meaning, of valency, of commitment, of

moral directive, shapes for us the significance of our selfhood. At first, our sense of meaning is not so much individual as communal. And from the awareness of the identity of the community in which we emerge, the reflexive sense of selfhood comes gradually aware of itself as mirrored in relationship with others and arriving at a sense of individuality. To regard ourselves as individuals is an achievement deriving from learning to look at ourselves from the perspective of others simultaneously with learning to experience ourselves in our own identity.

Once the stable sense of community, meaning, and self on these inarticulate levels has been achieved, meaning can move toward the articulate level. Certain actions take on symbolic significance, as when a parent's frown can shatter a child's sense of being approved. Through repetition of sounds and rhythms, through pictures and music, through the drive within us as children to respond to those speaking to us, we approach the threshold of speech.

Long before we have language, we have meaning. Before we can name its parts, we have acquired a world and a wholeness of experience. Yet we strive toward speech. And when we are able to participate in the language of our community on an articulate level, it is also with a sense of responding to what was there long before we arrived. "In learning to speak," writes Michael Polanyi, "every child accepts a culture constructed on the premises of the traditional interpretation of the universe, rooted in the idiom of the groups to which it was born, and every intellectual effort of the educated mind will be made within this frame of reference."[8]

Language as we learn it emerges from a rich background of tradition. And in learning it, we are confirmed in a complex and tacit dimension of meaning that has already been communicated to us in tactile ways, in the patterns of covenantal valencies, and in a wholeness of experiencing. Language relies upon this background, and its interpretation of particulars depends upon this comprehensive meaning.

Language is not acquired in order to create meaning. Language is an achievement, a hard-won social instrument for communicating meaning already present on an inarticulate level, but communicating it in greater detail, with more precision, and in order to serve better the purposes of control, differentiation, and innovation.

Language drifts toward triviality when we detach it from communal wholes of experiencing. Communally shared relations and meanings, covenantal passions and purposes, and the tactile and mythic elements of prelinguistic relation give birth to language and sustain it. A poem, therefore, with its rhythms and familiar sounds may give pleasure to a child before it understands the words accurately. Or the pleasure and meaning of a work of art may derive, not from knowing some literal meaning about it, but rather from participation in it as a mythic whole, a totality that cannot be articulated fully and that may be destroyed by attempts to reduce it to linguistic expression.

If language brings precision to our sense of community and self, then artistic perspective keeps us aware of the wholeness of experience. But the wholeness signifies more than aesthetic appreciation. It also means historical awareness, covenantal commitment, and the horizons of human believing.

3. History and Deity

As we seek to understand, to the limits of our capabilities, the mystery of human location, we discover that self-awareness emerges within a social, tactile context and that the fabric of selfhood is woven from the threads of human interaction in community. The socially constituted self is acted upon, acts in response, and meets new response, and by this means we encounter and become acquainted with the context of valuing, of moral demand, and of multiple loyalties that together comprise a field of communal meaning. The environment in which we emerge as selves is filled with power, charged with valencies of significance, and shaped by the covenants of our community of interpretation. Gradually the wholeness is interpreted to us. Vague and undefined confusion becomes patterned with particulars. We learn to speak in response to those around us, and we repeat the interpretations given us until we can imitate the words, follow the grammar, reproduce the music of verbal expression, and master the minutest detail of local accent. And as events are interpreted to us by companions around us in the continuing interaction of the community, we internalize the meaning, dwell in it, and exhibit it in our living.

Our horizons of meaning expand. "Just as the meaning of a sentence is more than that of all the naming words it contains," writes Herbert Richardson, "so the meaning of every story is more than that of all the sentences it contains."[9] As our selfhood emerges in community, we reach beyond the wholeness of our immediate surroundings toward wider meaning. We reach out into the mystery of our location for the story, now our story, that binds all the parts we encounter into a coherent whole and invests all particulars with significance. We join the community into which we are born with all the force of human believing in reaching toward history and toward God. "To be a self," H. Richard Niebuhr explains, "is to have a god; to have a god is to have history, that is, events connected in a meaningful pattern. . . . God and the history of selves in community belong together in inseparable union."[10]

Not only do we learn of our immediate environment within our community of interpretation, we also come to an understanding of the larger world of history and the comprehensive reality of believed-in deity. Through action and ritual, through story and myth, through formal and informal teaching, we acquire a sense of the past as it is remembered in our community, of the future as our companions anticipate it, of the present between past and future, and of convictions about the sovereign reality that gives meaning to the whole, informing all our interpretations and our actions. In the process of emerging into self-awareness, we arrive at the wholeness of historical consciousness that relates all the parts together into the meaning by which our community lives.

We are caught up also in the loyalties and meanings of our community. We are impelled toward commitment to its god or gods. The full dimensions of selfhood and human location are achieved only as we become aware of our history, with a sense of the relationship and coherence of events in our world, and as deity takes shape in our commitments and our actions.

In this perspective humans exist as selves directed toward deity in the elusive media of community and history. For this view, there can be no simple location among the bare facts of a crass empiricism, for it is only within the encompassing context of meaning given in communities of interpretation that experience is invested with pattern and definition. Only within community, with dimensions of historical awareness and horizons of reality, do selves have what can be called experience.

Once the outlines of this location are perceived, it also becomes clear that it is not an immovable, static place but a location in motion. Humans are afforded no Archimedean standpoint from which to understand with completeness and finality. The sources of our understanding are on the move and so are we. Human location, for all its mysterious quality, is an earthly location, not an ontological peak in a philosopher's heaven from which we may survey reality and describe it in absolute and final terms. Human location remains within the interpretive streams of remembering and hoping, of interaction in community.

Deity as it emerges in this perspective is not an object to be grasped and shifted about like cosmic furniture. No cosmonaut can gain a clearer view of deity by soaring farther from earth. Deity is believed in from earthly location, within communal traditions, as the horizon and medium of history. Deity is the comprehensive power believed in as linking events together in a meaningful whole, the sovereign reality of world occurrence, the power which, just as a magnet gives to iron filings the pattern of a magnetic field, shapes the fields of human commitments, loyalties, and actions. As selfhood provides a center of experience, so deity means the reality and the pervasive valency of experiencing.

In this view, gods can never be regarded only as static. Though they give order and stability to human worlds, gods are also dynamic and changing, for they appear to human believing in the shifting context of culture and history. The gods are multiple and changing, therefore, because there are many communities evolving through diverse histories. Even a deity believed in by a particular group as eternal and unchanging will change in the viewing and believing of that community as it encounters new situations and moves toward new societal patterns. When a global culture with diverse communities is emerging, it is inevitable that the gods reappear in their pluralism and their change. Disturbing as it may be for some theologians, they must come to recognize the dynamic aspect of deity. It is not only possible for theology to speak of changing gods today; it is necessary.

Recognition of human location as within history and deity means both limitation and possibility. Dwelling within these horizons, rather than in some metaphysical heights "outside" or "above" them, provides us with a perspective conditioned by our location.

Perspective is not an incidental element of human location. It is a constitutive condition of our existence. Without the particularities of place and the perspective that goes along with our being there, we have no human location. To the extent and in the ways that humans live and act, reflect and speak, remember and hope, they do so by virtue of particular social and historical locations, and on the basis of experiencing grounded in the perspective acquired in that location.

For many, the perspectival character of human viewing and thinking is a major defect in our world. Perspective is an epistemological flaw in systems of thought for these people, and so it must be concealed or denied. Many persons and communities attempt to ignore their location and pretend to an absolutism without perspective or to a perspective assumed to be absolute. Others, embarrassed by the admission that their thinking and their statements are conditioned by a particular perspective, try to argue their way out of the predicament: careful reasoning is universal and not subject to human location and perspective; a particular class is bearer of the absolute; a relatively unattached intelligentsia can view truth without the distortion of perspective; revelation exempts my community from the errors of perspective; or critical theory eliminates location and perspective.

Perspective does not seem to be a flaw or an embarrassment but a fundamental, constituting condition of human location. I am unable to understand my own experience if it is stripped of perspective. Nor can I understand how my fellow humans can claim to experience anything apart from their specific perspectives.

To have a particular location, to occupy a perspective, is not a disadvantage for humans. Instead it offers us the possibilities of a world in which to live and act. Perspective conditions our experiencing and at the same time opens a world before us. I cannot walk out of my house into all streets simultaneously. That is a limitation, but one which permits me to experience *that one street* with its blossoms in the spring, its old residents and new neighbors, to work on that street for my political party at election time, to comfort a friend whose daughter has died. Perspective gives me a world in which to work for justice, to ask for forgiveness, and perhaps to find love. Location provides pattern and specification and therefore makes being human real and possible for me.

Perspective threatens us, not when we admit it and develop its possibilities, but only when we think that we can escape it and that at last we have achieved a view of reality unencumbered by specific location and the perspective it provides. We are then unable to learn, for we do not suppose that there are any remaining possibilities beyond the horizons that we can see. We can no longer anticipate newness and the future, for we believe that we have grasped the pattern to which all time is subject. We can have no place in our lives for sympathy or empathy for others, for we have lost the ability to imagine worlds with meaningful perspectives different from our own. We can live in proximity to others, but not in love and understanding, for all views must conform to the truth as we know it or be rejected.

As the configuration of pluralism emerges in its theological significance, we begin to see with increasing clarity the differing communities of interpretation, the varied histories belonging to these communities, and the multiple gods informing their living. We begin to understand better the tradition and the faith that is ours. Perspective is no longer an embarrassment but the badge of our humanity as we dwell in a particular community, with its history and believed-in deity, within the encompassing mystery of human location.

PART TWO

PERSPECTIVE: PARADIGMS IN TRANSFORMATION

The old gods are growing old or are already dead, and others are yet to be born . . .

Emile Durkheim

God's self-disclosure is that permanent revolution in our religious life by which all religious truths are painfully transformed and all religious behavior transfigured by repentance and new faith.

H. Richard Niebuhr

VI.

THE DIS-EASE
OF WESTERN THEOLOGY

Announcing a conference of Catholic theologians several years ago, Karl Rahner made the striking observation that "theology is tired." At the time that I received the announcement, I was visiting a very energetic friend, who like Rahner is also a Catholic theologian. In response to Rahner's comment, my friend exclaimed to me, "It is not theology but Rahner that is tired!"

While there may have been some truth in this analysis, I cannot view the scene of contemporary theology in Europe and America without agreeing in part with Rahner. Western theology is clearly suffering from dis-ease. Is the problem, as Rahner suggests, that theology is merely tired? Or is theology on the verge of total exhaustion?

To those still under the spell of the past, the present problems are not serious but indicate only that we are in a period of temporary quiescence while we await the arrival of another Barth or Tillich or Niebuhr. To those overwhelmed by change, the dis-ease of theology is not a mild, temporary weariness but rather is a virulent malady portending the death of God, the end of religion, and the demise of the entire theological enterprise.

My own perspective on what is happening to theology has already been suggested. Though many obituaries have been written for God, religion, and theology, none is in danger of demise. Changing—yes; disappearing—no. The illness of theology is serious, but it is not a sickness unto death. Instead it is a debilitating ailment brought on by the inability of theology to gather resources for dealing adequately with the vast changes now taking place in human culture. Specifically, Western theology is caught between the currents of pluralism and the forces of liberation emerging now in global society. This dis-ease is made worse to the extent that contemporary theology finds it difficult to escape the ecclesiastical limitations of its past and to disentangle itself from the dichotomies endemic to the Western intellectual heritage. For these reasons, theology as practiced generally in Europe and America is undergoing a crisis of far-reaching significance.

The present illness of theology produces symptoms of anxiety and disorientation, rather than a high fever indicating an infection endangering the life of the patient. Instead of a mortal illness, theology is suffering from a *mal de mer,* a nausea, a dis-ease brought on by the growing recognition that humanity is in the midst of a voyage, that we are between a whence and a whither, and that we as humans are thrown together inescapably with other humans who have differing interpretations of the meaning of the voyage. Theology of the traditional, ecclesiastical variety is not merely tired. It is genuinely sick. But it is not on the verge of demise.

1. Theology in a New Cultural Situation

Placing the blame on conventional theologians for the current difficulties of Western theology is a fruitless enterprise. To do so would be much like finding fault with dinosaurs for becoming extinct when the environment changed.

Today there is a new situation brought on by the globalization of culture. The academic theology of North

Atlantic nations, ponderous in its massive scholarship, finds it difficult to respond to changing cultural conditions. Habits developed over 1600 years cannot be given up easily. The theological pattern that came to domination in the Constantinian era has governed theology during the long period of Christian ascendance—in western Europe during the Middle Ages and with global reach during the period of Western expansion—and has acquired an increasingly definite and settled structure. With limited variations, most theologians in the academic enclaves of Western culture have adhered to this paradigm and still adhere to it. Indeed, theological scholars often seem to be in conversation only with other theologians, working out minor in-group puzzles, rather than noticing or responding to what is occurring in the world around them.

In this century a dramatically different cultural situation has emerged, a situation in which organized Christianity is no longer dominant. The era of the Constantinian church is drawing to a close, and the theology based on the traditional pattern is in trouble. The paradigm dominant for the past millennium and a half is being shattered. Western theology of the older mode is moving toward extinction, and a transformed theology is taking shape.

This is not the first time that such a change has been necessary in Christian thought. An equally dramatic shift took place as the Christian movement emerged from its original status as a Jewish sect, moved into the different cultural situation of the Graeco-Roman world, and eventually became dominant in that wider milieu after the conversion of the Roman Emperor Constantine. The story of that theological transformation is worth telling in order to remind us that Christian thought has not always taken the form we call theology and that theology was not an exclusively Christian enterprise.

Christianity came into being as a minority movement in a distant corner of the Roman Empire. After three amazing centuries of growth, persecution, and further expansion, the Christian movement pervaded Roman society, had converted Constantine, and had become a legally sanctioned cult. By the time the Emperor Justinian closed the old pagan academies in A.D. 529, the position of Christianity had been consolidated even further into one of public religious monopoly. It is not surprising that profound changes in doctrine, governance, and practice took place in the Christian movement as it moved from isolated obscurity into a time of expansion and persecution and then into a position of power and dominance in the age of Constantine.

Christian thought initially took the form of telling stories of faith. "The preaching of the early Christian church," writes H. Richard Niebuhr, "was not an argument for the existence of God nor an admonition to follow the dictates of some common human conscience. . . . It was primarily a simple recital of the great events connected with the historical appearance of Jesus Christ and a confession of what had happened to the community of disciples."[1] This pattern for conveying Christian faith fits well in the cultural context within which the Christian movement emerged. Hebrew tradition and faith were communicated by dramatic recital of historic events, by telling the story of Israel's faith, by recounting the promises of God and their continuing fulfillment, and by cultic ritual acting out this history. Within this context of theology as story, specific teachings and moral directives acquired meaning and power. We may say, then, that the Christian movement inherited and continued the theological paradigm of the Hebrew tradition.

Christianity, however, moved out of the Jewish cultural sphere into the Graeco-Roman world, dominated politically by Rome and culturally by Athens. Though the Judaism within which Christianity was born had already been influenced by the surrounding hellenistic environment, the new movement was confronted by a pluralism and a variety of religious movements far beyond anything encountered in Galilee or Jerusalem. The theological paradigm that became closely associated with Western Christendom emerged gradually in the early centuries in response to the new cultural situation, just as the globalization of culture today requires response and is eliciting a new paradigm.

First among the forces reshaping Christian thought was Greek philosophy. Though theology itself is a Greek word and the earliest notion of theology as stories about the gods is similar to the conception the Christian movement inherited from its Hebraic background, it was the philosophy of Greece that played the more important role in transforming the ways of expressing Christian faith and shaping the emerging paradigm of theology. From as early as Justin Martyr on, Christian thinkers can be seen contending with Greek philosophy and absorbing its patterns. Clement of Alexandria writes, "The multitude are frightened at the Hellenic philosophy, as children are at masks, fearing lest it should lead them astray." Clement proposes to make full use of Hellenic philosophy in Christian thought. Yet, because "human speech is by nature feeble, and incapable of uttering God," dialectic cannot assimilate true wisdom "without the Savior, who withdraws, by the divine word, the gloom of ignorance arising from evil training, which had overspread the eye of the soul."[2] This pattern was given increasing definition by Lactantius, Origen, Athanasius, and especially by Augustine. The horizon of faith is provided by Scripture, but the substance, definition, and support are provided by rational, philosophical argument.

The second element shaping the new theological paradigm that emerged in the early centuries of the Christian movement is the institutional church as it became a powerful societal agency in the era after the conversion of Constantine. In this time, stable doctrine was needed. Rather than stories told by believers, theology gradually became the official dogmas defined by church councils and upheld by politically potent ecclesiastical organizations. Faith as right doctrine—orthodoxy, became more important than faith as trust and loyalty or as doing the will of God—orthopraxis. In the Constantinian era, theology became organizationally rationalized just as it became philosophically rationalized.

As this paradigm was articulated and adapted during the Middle Ages, these characteristics became more pronounced. Christianity in Europe came to occupy most of the cultural space, with Judaism and the remnants of heathenism and heresy relegated to the underside of society. It was not surprising that theology was thought of as an exclusively Christian enterprise and an enterprise that functioned within ecclesiastical dogma and space. Further, the reliance of theology on philosophy increased, first on Neoplatonic thought and then on Aristotelian philosophy. The hegemony of what we call the Constantinian paradigm of theology had become virtually complete.

The revolt of the Protestant reformers against medieval Catholicism appealed to the authority of the Bible in theology. Though their work did result in more emphasis on Scripture, especially in the life of the church, the theology of the different Protestant movements represented only variants of the traditional paradigm, not a shift to a new one. Much Protestant theology was as heavily dependent on philosophy as its medieval counterpart. Even that which explicitly rejected philosophy in favor of the Bible still followed the traditional paradigm in using a rationally discursive form for theological discourse rather than historical narrative and story as had been the case with the paradigm of theology governing the Bible and the early Christian movement. Just as decisively, the theology of the Protestant movements followed the Constantinian paradigm in regarding theology exclusively as a function of a particular ecclesiastical community.

This traditional paradigm has become even more entrenched in the academic theology of Western Christendom as European society has reached out around the globe during the past five hundred years. Because Christianity was indeed virtually the only form of institutional religion present in Europe and each Christian group tended to occupy its own territory, the aspect of the paradigm limiting theology to a single ecclesiastical community offered few difficulties during the centuries of Christian ascendancy. Theological habits were formed, however, that make it almost impossible for theologians to deal with the emerging global culture, which is characterized by pluralism and liberation.

It is a far cry from the Hebrew prophets, Paul, and Augustine, proclaiming their convictions in a context of multiple faiths, to the theologians of the nineteenth and twentieth centuries, confining their work to isolated academic faculties usually defined by the dogma of a particular denomination or confession. Western theology increasingly has become little more than varieties of church dogmatics. A dichotomy between church and world becomes its starting point, and the theological task becomes, first, to define the gospel, and second, to discover ways to proclaim it from theologians in the church to modern humans in the world.

In this ecclesiastical perspective, the proclamation of the gospel requires bridging a chasm between two separate spheres. Gerhard Ebeling expresses this view: "Christianity has become accustomed to existence in two places, the space of the church and the space of the world. We have become accustomed to two languages alongside one another, the Christian language with its venerable patina of two thousand years and the language of reality [sic!] impinging upon us."[3] Here are two spheres, two languages, and reality is assigned by Ebeling to what appears to be a version of Kant's phenomenal sphere. No wonder the problems of Christian communication and a new coming-to-language are so difficult. No wonder the relation of theology to reality is so enigmatic. The gospel becomes static, enshrined in the unreal language of Christian tradition, given over to our keeping, our preaching. Any dynamism present arises in our work of communicating from one sphere to another. God, in this bifurcated perspective, appears as a static, quiescent deity—in contrast to the storied God of the Bible continuously active and powerful in nature and history. And Jesus Christ, the Risen Lord, can be no stronger than the communications facilities of preachers, theologians, and ecclesiastical organizations. God becomes the deity of theological and ecclesiastical proclamation. The Resurrection is restricted to church dogma or to the realm of existential self-understanding and is reduced to retrospective debates over physical possibilities, metaphysical abstractions, and historical literalism.

Such ecclesiastical theologies have become inadequate today in at least two important respects. First, they are unable to provide conceptual tools for understanding biblical Christian faith and witnessing to its richness and power in the contemporary world. Second, they are unable to understand the multiple and changing gods of global culture and their significance for Christian faith. On the one hand, ecclesiastical theology is so entangled with a static view of tradition that it lacks the ability to relate the past creatively to the present and the emerging future. On the other hand, ecclesiastical theology makes it difficult if not impossible for the Judeo-Christian tradition, which in the past has been as enriched by encompassing other faiths as by maintaining its historical integrity, to encounter the amazing array of faiths disclosed by pluralism and engage in the creative interchange with them which is at the center of biblical mission.

Confronted by an altered cultural climate, Western theology has engaged in defensive maneuvers, intramural disputes, and bizarre fads in an effort to resist the pressures of the changing environment. For the most part, theologians have continued to follow the Constantinian paradigm, to shape their methods and concepts within the limits of the ecclesiastical organizations to which they belong, and to accept the intellectual presuppositions that have fostered the industrial and technological triumphs of Western society. Caught between pluralism and liberation, Western theology, it has become increasingly clear, has been on a collision course with the twentieth century. The result has been more and more stress, ever deeper problems. As Catholic neoscholasticism and Protestant neo-orthodoxy have been struck broadside by cultural change, and in particular by the movements of pluralism and liberation, we have been hearing around us the cries of the injured and the splintering of the theological timbers.

2. The Split World of Ecclesiastical Theology

Though the problems facing theology seem difficult, they do not arise because religious traditions and faiths are disappearing or because theology is no longer possible. Instead, the dis-ease of theology results from holding tenaciously to the past, adhering to the Constantinian paradigm, while the changing cultural context requires transformation.

It is not my purpose to praise or blame the past for being what it was. There were reasons for the emergence of ecclesiastical theology. My point here is that the Constantinian paradigm has been brought into crisis by events of this century. A new paradigm must be sought, and indeed appears to be taking shape. Let us trace the reasons for the crisis.

Not many generations ago, Western Christians and most of humanity around the world lived in socio-religious enclaves that had only marginal contact with one another. The views of self, companions, world, and God held by persons in these enclaves were shaped by their own particular "tribe" in relative isolation from other communities. People were aware that other tribes, other nations, other cultures, other religions existed, but the majority of individuals had little or no direct encounter with persons from other cultural enclaves. Elite minorities in positions of leadership had some contact with their counterparts in other cultures, but this was usually of a very limited character.

It is a decisive mark of the new cultural situation that this tribal isolation has been breaking down. The most rapid and dramatic movements out of social and religious isolation and toward multifaceted cultural encounter have taken place in the twentieth century. Increased mobility has done much to further the meeting of communities. Trains, motor cars, propeller aircraft, and now jets, transport more and more people with increasing rapidity across old boundaries into different cultures. The mass media have greatly extended and reinforced this meeting of diverse enclaves. Posters, newspapers, magazines, movies, radio, and television instruct humans in detail about what is going on in other cultural communities as well as in their own. The viewpoints, life-styles, economic and political conditions, and religious faiths of other nations and peoples become the daily fare of persons around the globe. The revolutions in travel and in communication have intensified the meeting of diverse cultures and have carried this encounter to all parts of the world, to almost every previously isolated human enclave, and into the tribal spaces and individual minds of everyone.

In this century, humanity is coming out of the traditional communities that limited persons to a single religious perspective and a coherent realm of societal loyalties. Humans today are being compelled to leave the secure custody of inherited dogmas and folkways. They are being thrust into a confusing context of differing faiths and conflicting commitments. Write Peter Berger and associates: "Through most of human history, individuals lived in life-worlds that were more or less unified. . . . Increasingly, as pluralization develops, the individual is forced to take cognizance of others who do not believe what he believes and whose life is dominated by different, sometimes by contradictory meanings, values, and beliefs."[4]

Marshall McLuhan has called this new cultural situation a global village. That is not adequate. When recognized in its full dimensions, it may be more accurately regarded as a global marketplace of competing loyalties, commitments, and faiths. We inhabit a developing worldwide society in which the diverse tribes of humanity meet in cultural commerce.

In this new situation, in addition to the meeting of cultures, the mounting pressure for liberation has been a no less dramatic and significant phenomenon. The age-old discontents of oppressed groups have voice and leadership and have been organized into powerful political movements. From the fifteenth century on, the rising tide of middle-class revolution altered the shape of Western societies. And the achievements of that revolution induced a revolution of rising expectations among exploited peoples everywhere. Lower socio-economic groups, excluded from the benefits of bourgeois affluence, clamored for their share and began organizing proletarian movements to gain their ends. A global revolt against colonialism brought scores of new nations into existence. Areas touched by the hopes but not the results of the middle-class revolution became the scenes of proletarian revolution. Ethnic and racial groups began protesting the wrongs done them and demanding economic and political rights. Women are refusing to accept second-class status and oppression by male-dominated societal structures. Peoples previously resigned to oppression have learned to hope and to rebel. The twentieth century has become the century of liberation as well as the era of the globalization of culture.

The twin phenomena of pluralism and liberation present Western theology with a different environment, a new cultural situation. The patterns of response guided by the Constantinian paradigm are no longer adequate. For example, the theology of Europe and North America comes from middle-class ecclesiastical contexts. As such, it is as troubled by movements of liberation as by pluralism. Wrote Walter Rauschenbusch: "Eminent theologians, like other eminent thinkers, live in the social environment of wealth and to that extent are slow to see."[5] The beneficiaries of the middle-class revolution, theologians as well as others, wish to retain their comforts; yet many feel guilty when confronted with the poverty and oppression under which the majority of the world's population still suffers. Marxism has lifted millions to a higher level of living but has left many forms of oppression untouched. The rising hopes for liberation continue to impinge painfully on the conscience of affluent Western Christianity.

The difficulties of the Constantinian paradigm come also from its acceptance of philosophical bifurcations. The Western intellectual tradition has long been characterized by assumptions that the world as experienced is divided into subjective and objective sectors (i.e. an epistemological bifurcation) and that there is a substantial or noumenal reality underlying what is experienced (i.e. a metaphysical bifurcation). These assumptions may be distinguished but are so closely intertwined as to be inseparable.

Many historians of Western thought trace these dichotomies back to Plato and to Neoplatonism. I regard this as a serious misunderstanding of platonic philosophy as found in the dialogues of Plato and an erroneous interpretation of the influence of Neoplatonism on Western theology. The major point of entrance of this split world into European thought is through the reintroduction of Aristotelian philosophy in the thirteenth century. Scholasticism, as the Aristotelian movement came to be known, has been an important form of Western thought since that time and has had great influence on most other forms. Problems perceived in this split world led to modifications and variations as modern philosophy and theology moved through the critical stage of their development. In the twentieth century, however, conditions and perspectives necessary for a post-critical era of thought have emerged.

The epistemological bifurcation appears in the Thomist presupposition that there is nothing in the mind that is not first in the senses, *nihil in mente non prius in sensu*. This formulation assumes a dichotomy between an inner or mental sphere and an external sphere, with the senses mediating between the two. The metaphysical bifurcation is also present in Scholasticism, for what appear in the senses are only phantasms or images of the external world that are not to be identified with the underlying substances that cause them. These bifurcations are held together by revelation, authority, and reason in Scholastic theology, which manages also to identify the dynamic Yahweh of the biblical heritage with the Unmoved Mover of Aristotelian philosophy.[6] However unlikely this mixture may seem, Scholasticism has remained among the most powerful forms of Western thought over the past seven hundred years.

Though Martin Luther attacked Aristotelian thought, Philip Melanchthon reintroduced scholastic rationalism. It carried the day in the development of Lutheran orthodoxy. As a consequence, Lutheranism has been compelled to wrestle ever since with such bifurcations as Law and Gospel, Nature and Grace, two kingdoms teaching, all of which reflect the epistemological and metaphysical splits of Scholasticism.

In Reformed theology, shaped by Bullinger and Calvin, Scholastic philosophy had little impact until the seventeenth century. Reformed communities, as a result, were able to produce the federal theologies of Olevianus and Cocceius, the federal political philosophy of Johannes Althusius, and the moral philosophy of Adam Smith, all of which exerted a profound influence on Western society and in which the traditional bifurcations play lesser roles.

Modern philosophy, often regarded as representing a radical break from Scholasticism, adopts the inherited bifurcations in a variant form. Descartes replaces theological authority with the method of doubt and critical reason, yet maintains the old epistemological and metaphysical bifurcations. John Locke, building on the scientific work of Isaac Newton, develops an impressive empirical analysis but reaffirms the split between inner and outer spheres and between the qualities of objects that produce sensory impressions and the underlying substance to which the qualities pertain. George Berkeley dispenses with the hazy notion of substance. For him the world is a vibrant tangle of sensory perception. Mind is not a subjective substance but is the activity of perceiving. At first, it appears that Berkeley has eliminated the split world, and indeed he must be accounted a brilliant forerunner of phenomenology. But Berkeley posits a Being underlying experience who is the source of the experienced universe, and the bifurcations are transposed into the theological problem of the existence of God.

David Hume combines a rigorous theoretic skepticism with a practical social believing, thus adding the theoretic/practical bifurcation to the Western intellectual tradition. Immanuel Kant, awakened from his dogmatic slumbers by Hume, builds upon this theoretic/practical distinction to produce a philosophic system that, in its originality, comprehensiveness, and influence, takes its place alongside the systems of Plato, Aristotle, and Plotinus. Kant reformulates the old metaphysical bifurcation and posits two realms, the phenomenal realm of appearance and the noumenal realm of things-in-themselves. The phenomenal realm is accessible through the sensory manifold to theoretic reason, which can, as in the natural sciences, arrive at precise statements. But the work of theoretic reason pertains only to the realm of phenomena and reaches beyond itself if it attempts to make statements about the noumenal realm. Only to human awareness in practical reason and in teleological judgment, that is, to humans as decision-making, planning, believing agents, is the noumenal accessible.

Philosophy since Kant has been largely variations on Kantian themes, and Protestant theology in Europe and North America can be regarded as a series of footnotes to Kant. The traditional paradigm of Western theology took a Kantian form for Protestants as decisively as it took a Thomistic form for Catholics. Emphasizing first one and then another aspect of Kant's philosophy, theologians adjusted themselves to a world split into phenomenal and noumenal realms and into theoretic and practical reasoning.

Liberal theology utilized the Kantian bifurcations as a means to accept natural science and the rationalism of the Enlightenment, yet at the same time leave room for faith. Friedrich Schleiermacher, who became deeply attracted to Kant's thought after he smuggled a forbidden *Critique of Theoretic Reason* into the Moravian seminary he was attending and read it behind drawn drapes, reflects the dichotomies of critical philosophy. G. F. W. Hegel, as much philosophical theologian as theological philosopher, starts with the Kantian division but sees subjective and objective reason lifted up dialectically and united in Absolute Spirit or God. Existentialists, from Søren Kierkegaard forward, entered into the practical side of Kant's thought, imaginatively expanded the inward ground of faith, and widened the split between subjective self-understanding and the objective world of factual occurrence.

Suspicious of both liberalism and existentialism, Karl Barth developed neo-orthodoxy by emphasizing the self-proclamation of God in Jesus Christ through the church. In so doing, he contrasts the phenomenal realm of human religious grasping after the ungraspable God with the noumenal realm of God breaking in upon human consciousness by means of revelation and creating the faith by which God is received.

Though many regard Barth as a point of decisive change in twentieth century theology, a view informed by the history of philosophy discloses his continuity with the predecessors he so roundly denounced. As Richard R. Niebuhr reminds us:

Two thinkers so widely separated as Ludwig Feuerbach and Karl Barth treat essentially the same theme, the life of practical reason. . . . Consequently, while the academic theology of Protestantism in the last quarter century has often been described as a revolt against its antecedents, that is true only in a superficial sense. . . . [Barth's *Römerbrief*] is, after all . . . not a cancellation of the line whose course must be plotted from Kant through Schleiermacher, Hegel, Strauss, Feuerbach, the Tübingen school and Ritschl, as well as through the lecture hall of 1900 in which the text of *Das Wesen des Christentums* was originally delivered.[7]

In this perspective, it becomes apparent that neo-orthodoxy does not represent a rejection of the past in two important respects. First, it continued the dichotomies of Western thought, took them to radical theological conclusions, and thereby hastened the crisis of a theological paradigm based upon a split world. Second, neo-orthodoxy continued the well-established tradition restricting theology to the Christian ecclesiastical sphere. Indeed, neo-orthodox theology makes it clear that intellectual bifurcations and ecclesiastical limitations reinforce one another.

Acceptance of the metaphysical and epistemological bifurcations of the philosophical tradition, with their presupposition of a gnosis hidden from ordinary human perception, fits well with a theology limited to an ecclesiastical area, where divine truth is revealed, split off from ordinary human space. By accepting this trinity of bifurcations (metaphysical, epistemological, ecclesiastical), Western theology has gradually withdrawn from the larger cultural arena into sectarian communities, retreated from the wider intellectual market place into academic enclaves, and narrowed its concern from human need and aspiration to issues of churchly survival and propriety. As a result, theologies of the Constantinian paradigm have been thrown into crisis.

3. Theology in Crisis

Among the clearest symptoms of the profound dis-ease affecting Western theology and ethics are the varied fads of recent decades. But these bizarre movements are only extreme examples of the stress and strain evident in all theological reflection governed by the Constantinian paradigm.

Indications of trouble in Western theology are not new. For example, we may name the modernist controversies in Catholic and Protestant Christianity earlier in this century or the confusions surrounding the proposal for "demythologizing" the Bible. The difficulties hit the headlines in 1963 when Bishop John A. T. Robinson published *Honest to God*. The little book became an instant best seller in England and was soon evoking discussion in America, on the European continent, and around the world. In particular, Robinson offers a simplified account of issues raised by Rudolf Bultmann, Dietrich Bonhoeffer, and Paul Tillich. More generally, he is asking whether inherited patterns of theology and ethics are adequate for our time.

Robinson points to the outmoded language of churches and theologians, to the isolation of theology in ecclesiastical spheres, and to the need for some "radical recasting [of] . . . the most fundamental categories of our theology."[8] He sees Bultmann, Bonhoeffer, and Tillich wrestling helpfully with these problems. Yet Robinson, along with his theological examples, for the most part continues to accept the bifurcated world of the Western intellectual tradition, and he identifies himself from the outset as an earnest guardian and defender of Christian truth as set forth in the Anglican Book of Common Prayer. He remains firmly within the Constantinian paradigm, even as he articulates its problems.

As it turned out, *Honest to God* was the forerunner of an incredible procession of theological fads. Best known among these are the "secular theology" and the "God-is-dead" movements.

The secular theology movement had a praiseworthy aim in attempting to shift the attention of Christians from another world to the realities of this world. One may even be moved by the pious purpose of secular theology to rescue Jesus from his unfortunate entanglements with a supernatural deity. Nevertheless, as the movement appears in its popularized forms, it is caught in the split world that it rejects yet continues to presuppose and in ecclesiastical limitations which it still accepts.

First, the secular theologians intend to reject other-worldliness and supernatural metaphysics. Yet the use of the term secular continues to assume the bifurcated world of the sacred/secular dichotomy that is supposedly discarded. In addition, each of these thinkers wants to maintain something equivalent to the discarded sacred within the secular sphere. The result is confusing and contradictory. On the one hand, "Secularization is man turning his attention away from worlds beyond and toward this world and this time," writes Harvey Cox, and "secularization represents 'objective reality.' " On the other hand, he insists that the church is "the avant-garde of the new regime," and *only faith can discover the Church of Jesus Christ.*"[9] Cox combines Kant, Comte, and Barth into a strange, uneven mixture.

Second, the meaning of the secular remains confused. Paul van Buren asks: "How can a Christian who is himself a secular man understand the Gospel in a secular way?" At one point he seems to identify this secular stance as "the reaction to the Idealism of the last century"; at another point, secularism appears to be equated with empirical verification; and later, he regards himself as a secular man because of his "commitments to modern science." None of these taken alone is satisfactory. Together they are neither clear nor consistent. What remains clear for van Buren is Jesus, understood through the Easter proclamation. "When Easter is in the center . . . we can say that the meaning of the Gospel is to be found in the areas of the historical and ethical, not in the metaphysical or the religious."[10] And so the secular meaning of the gospel becomes an echo of Bultmann and a bit of warmed-over Kant. After these treatments by Cox and van Buren, it is small wonder that some regard the "secular" as the longest oblong blur in recent theology.

Third, the secular theologians still view the secular

from an ecclesiastical perspective. They thus become incapable of recognizing the rich and varied texture of human believing present in the cultural sectors they indiscriminately lump together as secular. Believing is still defined by traditional ecclesiastical space, and the multiple and changing gods of global culture are rendered invisible.

Of equal importance as a symptom of theological dis-ease is the "God-is-dead" movement—with its excellent press, its intriguing imagery, its historical and conceptual confusions, and its consequent lack of clarity as to which deity is deceased and the time and circumstances of the death. In some cases, it appears that adherents of this movement have followed Ludwig Feuerbach and reduced theology to a peculiar kind of anthropology. In this perspective, we may see humanity, suitably costumed for the cosmic stage, enclosed in a vault of existential terminology, and rouged over for projection onto a heavenly screen, put forward as substitute for deceased deity. A dead God then only represents the projection of a dead humanity. Perhaps it is this specter that has led many to conclude that it is theology, not God, that is dead.

The theme of God's death in varied guises is an old one. It appears in Job, in the mystery religions, in the development of Christology, in Martin Luther and John Calvin, in Wolfgang Goethe, William Blake, Hegel, Feuerbach, Dostoyevsky, and Nietzsche, to name a few. The notion of the death of God can have a variety of meanings: Ingmar Bergman's "silence of God"; the end of an otherworldly, objectified idea of deity; the death of faith; the fading of old symbols and outmoded language; the killing of God again and again through human lovelessness; or the orthodox truism that God in Jesus Christ is crucified and dead.

To make any sense of this fad, the death of God must be understood as poetic protest. As outcry, as protest against sham piety and phony faith, the death of God can be heard as biblical witness. In this perspective, the

God-is-dead movement was not radical enough. Until we know God as void and as enemy, we cannot come to know God as companion and redeemer. The image of the death of God may therefore be a powerful image that can deceive us into the truth of the gospel.

When this has been said, however, it is necessary to recognize that the fad of the sixties lacked this depth of perception about itself. It made good publicity because it shocked a religious and theological public informed by the split world of ecclesiastical theology. But the death-of-God faddists were too hypnotized by their own outrageous slogan (and perhaps also by the public attention they received) to reach for new symbols by which we might see the world anew and move beyond the bifurcated reality they still postulated.

This passage from Gabriel Vahanian, a theologian who combined the secular and death-of-God motifs, illustrates the confused concepts of these confusing movements. "Because God is the creator and because his creation is not divine, the Bible holds that true secularity is the only religious mode of being; and by not separating the secular from the religious it also affirms, so to speak, that the secular is the real and the real is the religious."[11] This kind of theological nonsense can be written because the old, Constantinian paradigm still governs these theologians, even as they recognize its inadequacy for the new cultural context.

Whatever the differences among the theologians of secularization and divine decease, they have one fascinating area of agreement. Beneath their gaudy gowns of mass-media phrasing, a tattered slip of ecclesiastical faith is showing. They retain a touching piety toward Jesus. And it lends to their endeavors an air of medieval piety rather than the hard-nosed modernity to which they pretend. They still dwell in the split world of ecclesiastical theology. And so they illustrate, not the secularity of our world or the death of God, but rather the crisis of conventional theology confronted by pluralism and liberation.

Robinson's *Honest to God* also has a chapter on "The New Morality," in which he demonstrates that his understanding of ethics is no better than his grasp of theology. Even so, he reminds us that ethics is also caught in the crisis of the Constantinian paradigm.

In the new morality, Robinson tells us, nothing is prescribed except love. He quotes with approval from an article by Joseph Fletcher. "Christian ethics is not a scheme of codified conduct. It is a purposive effort to relate love to a world of relativities through a casuistry obedient to love."[12] This article was later expanded into a book[13] and launched the situation-ethics, or new-morality, fad of the sixties.

Parallel to the secular and God-is-dead theologies, this movement in ethics is attempting to throw off an outmoded past—old moral directives and ethical language—on behalf of attention to the real world around us, viewed in the fresh perspective of love. But the situationist movement stumbles in the same way as do the theological fads over its traditional presuppositions. It still operates within the Constantinian paradigm.

First, situation ethics can safely reject codes and presuppose pragmatism, relativism, positivism, and personalism because the "situation" is Constantinian, with organized Christianity dominant and supported by societal authority. Second, situation ethics can afford to be vague about the meaning of love because it assumes ecclesiastical location, where love means Christian love, explained in stories of faith and exemplified in Jesus. Third, situationism, with its dichotomies between situation and rule, love and law, and the like, remains in the split world of Western thought. It is still governed and limited by the traditional paradigm.

Such a perspective cannot deal with a pluralistic cultural context in which fundamental norms clothed with political power are in conflict. Nor can a bourgeois situationism be adequate when confronted with demands for liberation that require redistribution of societal access and goods. It is the clash of perspectives appearing within the context of the globalization of culture that is creating moral dilemmas today. In such a situation, situation ethics seems limited and thin.

It is not only in theological ethics that the stress and strain of the Constantinian paradigm appear. The rational ethics of fairness as argued with detailed brilliance by John Rawls depends upon a society governed by middle-class norms and a secure academic enclave in which he can work and be understood. And Kai Nielsen, in his *Ethics Without God*, operates with concepts governed no less by the Constantinian paradigm than the most ecclesiastical of ecclesiastical theologians—though with somewhat different purposes.[14]

Theological fads did not end with the sixties. David Miller jumped on the bandwagon of polytheism, which William Hamilton tried to get going in his post-death-of-God period. An alumna of Esalen and *est* helped Tom Driver find his genitals and thus assisted in launching the body theology fad. Now it is possible that a new fad is on the way: orthodoxy. The symptoms of theological dis-ease and crisis continue to appear.[15]

In *Honest to God*, Robinson correctly perceived that the issues of secularity and religionless religion, of the death of God and being for others, are of German provenance. A continuing problem of theology in the United States has been that all too often it has given more attention to continental movements than to what is going on in theology and society on this side of the Atlantic. German theologians for the most part are isolated in university theological faculties, enclosed within the Teutonic cultural sphere, and imprisoned within the European intellectual tradition. They are usually removed from the realities of parish concerns and of human living in ordinary society. And their work is more representative of the Constantinian paradigm than is the varied theological scene here. The many theologians in the United States, who divide themselves into academic cliques, following one or another German scholar of theology or biblical studies, and argue only with each other in print and in professional meetings about

European issues, are therefore twice removed from reality. The wag who said, "When German theology sneezes, American theology catches pneumonia," has gone far in explaining the peculiar theological fads of the sixties.

While the excesses of the American scene cannot be blamed on Europe, there clearly are connections. Rudolf Bultmann's existentialism, his emphasis on preaching, his confusion on the subject of mythology, and his dependence on Heidegger's philosophy, illustrate his adherence to the Constantinian paradigm and suggest his relationship to American theological fads. Karl Barth's location of theology within the ecclesiastical sphere, his declaration of revelation as the abolition of religion, and a conception of deity heavily dependent upon Kant places Barth also in the background of theological vagaries in the United States. Friedrich Gogarten's program of secularization and Dietrich Bonhoeffer's oft misunderstood rejection of religion in a world coming of age have been German sneezes that have contributed to the theological pneumonia across the Atlantic. All these theologians are working within the traditional pattern of theology, some of them recognizing and wrestling with its difficulties more than others. Their theologies remain caught within the split world of their European past and do not escape ecclesiastical limitations.

We must give credit to theologians of the past, Germans as well as others, for seeking to respond faithfully to God within their own context. In particular we are indebted to the existential and neo-orthodox theologians of this century for resisting the tendency to reduce the God of biblical faith to an item in the natural or phenomenal series. But the means they have used, seeming to limit God to the noumenal realm with such terminology as "wholly other," the Subject who is never Object, existential self-understanding in faith, and Ground of Being, are scarcely more attractive. If various naturalisms transformed deity into a supernatural magician, these theological reactions threaten to reduce

God to an existential or dogmatic ghost in the cosmic machine.

If we are to avoid being confronted with these unhappy alternatives, we must escape the bifurcated world of the Western intellectual heritage and the restrictions of ecclesiastical method. A paradigm adequate for theology in the emerging era must forge new concepts and methods. This theological pattern cannot be derived from inherited dichotomies but rather from the integral, active wholeness of human experiencing. Its scope cannot be limited to a single ecclesiastical enclave but must have as its horizon the whole of creation as reflected in a global culture characterized by pluralism and liberation.

VII.

RELIGION AND CHANGE

Alice in Wonderland, read with pleasure by children and adults alike, offers much that is instructive for those who wish to understand human believing. At one point, Alice is lost. She meets the Cheshire Cat and asks anxiously, "Would you tell me, please, which way I ought to go from here?"

"That depends a good deal on where you want to get to," the cat quite sensibly replies.

"I don't much care where," says Alice.

"Then," concludes the cat, "it doesn't matter which way you go."

When there is uncertainty about one's location and destination, the right way to go is indeed hard to find. Add confusion about ultimate commitments and believed-in gods, and the disorientation becomes total. If the current dis-ease of Western theology is a lostness (like Alice's) within a shifting world, then a central issue for religious faith is the meaning of change. We must discover how to keep a sense of direction in a time when, to use Ernst Troeltsch's phrase, *Es wackelt alles,* "Everything is shaking."

On all levels of human experience, culture is in process of change and people are confronting traditional viewpoints with a sense of loss. The scientific revolution has set humans adrift in the vastness of the physical and biological universe. The technological revolution has set persons adrift in a world of mobility and exploding information (and misinformation). Revolutions in the political economy have set entire peoples adrift in societal instability. Now a religious revolution is setting humanity adrift in a world of pluralistic meanings. The gods are reappearing, competing, and changing. Everywhere, in all societies, the walls protecting the old religious enclaves are being breached; humans and their communities are being evicted from the homelands of inherited faith. How, if at all, can change and religion be seen as related?

As new cultural vistas have opened humans to global perspectives, differing interpretations of the relation between religion and change have been put forward. One widespread view regards change as the enemy of religion. Change dissolves faith and overcomes religion. Religion is a phase of human experience that is fading away and being replaced by other activities or modes of thought. Some are pleased that this is occurring and welcome higher, clearer, more rational ways of interpreting experience. Others regret the disappearance of religion and look back with nostalgia to a past when faith seemed sure and simple.

A second view regards change neither as good nor bad but as the inescapable condition of human living that offers possibilities for creative thrusts of human believing toward an unfolding future of liberation. In this perspective, dynamism and becoming are as much a part of human believing as continuity. Change is a constitutive element of all human understanding of God and therefore also of all theology and ethics. There is, then, hope as well as peril in change.

Much writing about religion today takes the first of these views. As a result, the element of nostalgia is strong, and religion takes on a static appearance to be spoken of always in the past tense. When one takes the second view, however, and explores its implications carefully, a fascinating understanding of religious believing and its role in human living emerges.

WHEN GODS CHANGE

1. No Direction Home?

Early in the 1960s Bob Dylan, the folk singer, sang joyfully "The times they are a'changing." But a few years later, his tone had become one of uncertainty and nostalgia. "How does it feel / To be on your own / With no direction home?" Faced with the situation of pluralism and change, many feel lost and on their own and seek escape in longing for times and circumstances of a remembered past. They want to find the way back home.

Nostalgia in the face of change is not new. Mircea Eliade tells us that the myths of primitive peoples are saturated with nostalgia. In the myth and its reenactment in religious ritual, an original time is recreated that depicts the creation, recites the story of the gods, and provides a paradigm for human action in all important spheres of living. Such myths, writes Eliade, represent "the nostalgia for the perfection of beginnings."[1]

Romantics in every age have pined for a past that they supposed was unified and did not have the confusing complexity of the present. The *philosophes* of the eighteenth century Enlightenment looked back to the clear rationality of the classical era and deplored the obfuscating superstitions of the Middle Ages and Reformation. Aesthetes of the nineteenth century like Henry Adams wistfully sought a return to the illusory unity of medieval times and denounced the barren diversity of a society shaped by Protestantism and industrialism. Thomas Wolfe adds a note of poetic hopelessness to this nostalgia in his novel, *You Can't Go Home Again:* "Which of us is not forever a stranger and alone? . . . O lost, remembering speechlessly, we seek the great forgotten language, the lost lane end into heaven. A stone, a leaf, an unfound door."

In its political forms, nostalgia may turn into pessimism: the West is declining; the environment has been irreparably damaged, and humanity is doomed; the corporate devils of capitalism have made all bourgeois societies evil; or communists are everywhere destroying our beautiful world of automobiles and television. In this interpretation, with all its variations left and right, every present age is a time of decline and disintegration.

Nostalgia produces also a variety of responses. Sometimes nostalgic pessimism leads to violence. By means of nostalgia, many today excuse themselves from responsibility for changing the existing order and making the world somewhat better than it was in the past. Others become apologists for repression and cruelty on behalf of a nostalgic ideal.

In the perspective of nostalgia, religion is reduced to the past tense, and it is only the religious faith of a past time which can provide humans with a homeland. Religion to be authentic must be backward looking and resistant to social change. Because pluralism undermines the faith inherited from the past, it turns us into orphans with no direction home. One group of social scientists holding this view writes:

Pluralization weakens the hold of religion on society and on the individual. . . . The final consequence of all this can be put very simply (though the simplicity is deceptive): *modern man has suffered from a deepening condition of homelessness.* The correlate of the migratory character of this experience of society and of self has been what might be called a metaphysical loss of "home." It goes without saying that this condition is hard to bear. It has therefore engendered its own nostalgias—nostalgias, that is, for a condition of "being at home" in society, with oneself, and, ultimately, in the universe.[2]

Even the distinguished social philosopher, Daniel Bell of Harvard, with the superficial view of history and faith characteristic of many social scientists, asks, "What holds one to reality, if one's secular system of meanings proves to be an illusion?" And he responds, "I will risk an unfashionable answer—the return in Western society of some conception of religion. . . . What religion can restore is the continuity of generations, returning us to the existential predicaments which are the ground of humility and care for others."[3]

WHEN GODS CHANGE

The theme is that of return to the past. There can be no direction home except the way back to the religion of the past. Humans must resist change and cling to the dogmas which, it is supposed, gave our ancestors a sense of home.

Do we really want to return to the past? Do we want to go back to the time when slavery was upheld by the secure religious homeland of the slaveholders? Do we really wish to return to times not so long ago when the overwhelming majority of humans lived in abject poverty, oppressed by a tiny minority of nobility, royalty, and their god? Do we wish to abandon the hard won liberations of recent centuries in order to reenter what some believe was a cosmic home?

Put another way, is the primary function of religion to make us feel secure? Is religious faith to be understood as the static background of human living against which change can be measured—and resisted? Many wish to interpret religion in this way.

Perhaps the problem of homelessness arises in human consciousness, *not* because we cannot find our way back to an imagined homeland of the past, but rather because we refuse to recognize that our own home cannot be identical with the one that our parents or grandparents occupied. Our task is to make a home of the place in which we now live. "All homes," writes William James, "are in finite experience; finite experience as such is homeless."[4] This lesson has not been learned by those nostalgic souls who are tormented by the homelessness of modern humanity. They are like the young man who complained, "My father got to marry my mother, but I must go out and marry a perfect stranger."

When we look wistfully toward the past, our questions are wrong, and we are unable to read the road signs that might give us guidance. There is no direction home by way of nostalgia. Our homeland is around us and ahead. We cannot orient ourselves in the present by peering anxiously at a receding vision of the past. The direction of our looking must be changed, not to forget our past, but to live *where we are now* as responsible humans seeking to shape this present toward a homeland of liberation. The past can become a preoccupation used to escape the problems of the present.

"Nowadays," José Pintauro suggests, "to be on your way is to be home."[5] Religious faith, then, does not refer to a static past but rather is like a compass in the earth's magnetic field. It represents the response of humans to the encompassing reality in which they live. As present activity of believing, religious faith provides humans with a sense of orientation and location that can make of every journey a home.

But some observers insist that religion is doomed to extinction if it cannot fulfill nostalgic longings for the supposed security of our childhood. Religion, it is said, is dissolving into the surrounding context of what is vaguely called the "secular." In spite of persuasive arguments, there is also reason to doubt this view.

The opinion that religion is declining into oblivion appears to be as old as religion itself. It can be found among the ancient Egyptians and Babylonians and in the Graeco-Roman world. It reappears in all ages in differing forms and under varying auspices. It is perhaps a never-ending hope of those who oppose the prevailing forms of organized religion and an enduring fear of those who favor those forms but lack confidence in their power.

After the American Revolution and the creation of the United States of America, state-established religion was gradually ended. Both the rationalists who opposed Christianity and nervous church leaders predicted that the churches would disappear. Neither the hopes of the former nor the fears of the latter were confirmed. Cut loose from state support and dependent on voluntary membership, organized religion underwent incredible expansion. In 1790 only 5 percent of a population of four million in the United States belonged to churches. By 1960 over 64 percent of a population of nearly two hundred million belonged to churches; according to public opinion polls, an even larger percentage regarded themselves as related to a religious organization.

Quite clearly, religion did not disappear in America. The dangers to Christianity have been of a different nature. Not extinction, but success and assimilation to national purposes and societal values have been the real perils.

The evidence from the United States does not confirm the view that religion is disappearing, nor does the expansion of Christianity around the globe over the past four centuries. A revitalized Islam also has been gathering renewed strength in lands where it had long been dormant and has become a major competitor of other faiths in the new nations of Africa and Asia. Old and new forms of Hinduism and Buddhism have been expanding and exhibiting signs of new vitality in Asia and in the Western world. And it is difficult to exclude the emergence and dynamic growth of that new and powerful faith, Marxism, in its variant forms. The evidence against the position that religion is disappearing seems overwhelming.

Nevertheless, I am inclined to agree in part with the advocates of religious decline. But I agree from a quite different angle of vision.

Religious faith as the ultimate dimension of human commitment and believing is, I am convinced, a pervasive characteristic of human living. There is, however, no religious "essence," no static, unchanging entity that can be defined once and for all as "religion." Particular forms of human believing are indeed declining, and some are disappearing. But they are being replaced by other faiths.

Once we rid ourselves of the temptation to *define* religion and to judge its presence or absence by that one static pattern, human believing is disclosed as changing but in no way disappearing. It is constantly shifting, declining, coming into view again in different, often amazing, forms. Like a kaleidoscope, the hues and patterns alter, but the rich texture of color remains. Sometimes religious change takes place slowly, at other times rapidly, sometimes quietly, at other times with dramatic power. Each human generation, society, and individual must come to its own faith, and that faith can no more be identical with the faith of the ancestors or of another societal group than can the individuality of living entities be identical. "Everyone must do his own believing," said Martin Luther, "just as he must do his own dying."

When we are able to recognize the changing forms of religious faith, we discover that we are not observing the disappearance of faith or the demise of religion. Instead, we are witnessing the age-old occurrence of the changing of the gods.

In this illuminating perspective, we can make a startling discovery about the relation of religion and change. Religious believing, in individuals and in communities, is never static. Indeed, humans dwell in their faith most fully, not in order to hold on to the past, but as a means to break out toward the future. Religious faith is a transaction between environment and human believing by means of which humans maintain a sense of stability and location, that is, discover their ever-emerging homeland, while they are on the never-ending journey from the past into the future. Religion and change are not enemies but partners in the unfolding saga of humanity and deity. The end of religion is its constant transformation and renewal. In all its changing wonder, religious believing does have an end; but it is an end that is not its *finis* but its *telos,* not its extinction but its purpose.

2. Change as Theological Phenomenon

Once we have altered our angle of vision and recognized change and religious believing as symbiotic, then it becomes clear that theological reflection must be responsive to both. The task of theology is not to record static dogma from the settled past but rather to participate in humanity's constant wrestling with ultimate issues. Change is as much a theological as a human phenomenon.

WHEN GODS CHANGE

Theological change takes place in relation to three levels of human experiencing: the societal level, the level of comprehensive commitment and believing, and the ultimate level of believed-in deity/reality. Change on any of these levels, as they fall within the scope of theological endeavor, will be reflected in theological change.

The notion of society directs our attention to the patterns of human interaction. Included are those moral directives specifying approved and disapproved behavior. Included also are the rituals that channel action and inculcate group values. Religious believing points to the traditions and comprehensive commitments of societal entities that provide a context of faith to explain, legitimate, and reinforce societal directives and rituals. Deity or reality refers to the ultimate level of what is believed in as valuable and actual. Gods thus provide the validating power governing societal interaction and religious commitments. The work of theology and ethics takes place within these encompassing fields of force as persons wrestle with the ultimate issues of value and actuality as they arise with reference to proximate, specific problems. Theology operates on that boundary between the traditions from the past, which provide stable norms for human activity, and the changing convictions about deity and reality, which are reshaping religious believing and societal action. To examine the relation of religion and change for theology, we must explore the significance of change on each of the three levels.

Social change, rapid and seemingly irreversible, looms large in every sector of human experience. Expanding technological power and a culture developing toward global horizons are unfolding before our eyes. In spite of the modern mania for the new, it has become clear that the results of change are highly ambiguous. It produces benefits, but it also brings perils, some known, others yet to be revealed. In the process of social change, oppressions from the past are overcome but new forms of oppression emerge into view. As the human environment expands outward toward galactic space and inward toward the microcosms of consciousness and organic process, the ambivalent possibilities of change become ever more apparent.

Human capabilities increase so that we now travel faster, communicate more quickly, heal more ailments, harness greater power, manufacture more goods. At the same time, the four horsemen of the modern apocalypse—poverty, population, pollution, and oppression—stifle human potential everywhere and threaten the existence of the human community. Though human achievements stagger the imagination, we seem to be losing the struggle for justice and peace in the world.

As the dilemmas of change become clear, the task of theology and ethics in its social dimensions emerges. The continuing work of theology is to forge new tools for understanding the shifting social scene in its most comprehensive dimensions and to develop criteria to guide human communities in active response to change. Even if theology could evade alteration of its overall structure and method, continuing change would still be inescapable since a changing social context calls for responses that fit the problems rather than repetition of old answers to outmoded questions.

Not only does society change, so also does religious faith. In one way, change in religious faith is a well-known phenomenon in the form known as conversion. Persons may change from one faith to another; such change has even been known to happen to entire tribes or peoples. Theology is on familiar terms with conversion but not so accustomed to change of other kinds.

The most cursory review of the major religious traditions in all human cultures reveals a record of continuing upheaval. The Hebrew-Christian heritage illustrates this tendency: the Exodus movement recounted in the saga of Moses, the transformations brought about by the prophets of Israel and Judah, the new directions initiated by Jesus and Paul, the movements of reform in the

Catholic Middle Ages and the Protestant Reformation, and the responses to change in the modern world from the theologians of the nineteenth century to the Second Vatican Council of the 1960s. This is hardly a history of stasis. So characteristic is change of the Christian experience that H. Richard Niebuhr has described life in the community of Christian faith as "permanent revolution."

Oriental religious development also provides illustrations of changing patterns of religious commitment. The Aryan invasion into the Indus Valley, the emergence of Hinduism, and the transformation of that faith by means of the *Upanishads* suggest the scope and direction of an entire era on the Indian subcontinent. The emergence, or reemergence, of Jainism in the sixth century B.C. suggests both a major change and a different direction of development, as does the rise of Buddhism around the same time. There are continuing changes in each of these traditions, including the eventual movement of Buddhism out of India into other Asian lands. Further change came with the incursion of Moslems into India and the establishment of a strong Islamic movement there. The prophetic leadership of Mahatma Gandhi demonstrates that vitality and change have continued within the Indian culture. The Indian religious experience can in no way be regarded as static.

The heritage of China is still another source of illustrations of religious change: the renewal of China's ancient religion by means of Confucianism; the development of the mystical faith of Taoism; the penetration of Buddhism into China; the new forms of these old faiths; the emergence of a dynamic and powerful Maoism; and most recently the reevaluation of Mao and a possible turn toward a new Confucianism. China is a scene of dramatic religious change.

Change in the patterns of theological reflection within each tradition has accompanied and been a part of all these instances of religious change. And because the human believing which shapes religion is set within a context of historical circumstances and particularity, social and cultural changes are always symbiotically interrelated with changing comprehensive commitments for theology.

If religion is subject to change and even revolution, why does it appear to many observers as resistant to change and as a force working to maintain the status quo? An obvious answer to this question is possible when one considers how narrowly religion is ordinarily conceived, even by scholars. Identification of religion with its institutional forms both conceals changes going on within a particular religious movement and obscures new movements of faith that may revive or shatter traditional patterns. When only existing static forms of religion are taken into account, religious change cannot be recognized until it has already been accomplished and again become institutionalized. There is no way, on that basis, to anticipate change or to observe it as it occurs. Only as conceptual reform takes place can theology take account of change in a conscious, directed way rather than recording only the outcomes of prior religious change.

As reflection on religion and as the wrestling of religious faith with ultimate issues arising in new forms, theology cannot do other than respond to change. Theologians live on the moving boundary between past and future. They can, therefore, no more detach themselves from the remembering, which provides continuity with the past, than from the anticipating, which is the moving face of the future in every present. Theology, responding to changing socio-religious contexts, has undergone change in the past and will continue to do so.

3. Deity and Change

While Paul Tillich was teaching at Harvard University in the 1950s, a doctoral student in philosophy accused him of practicing theological fraud. The basis of this charge was that Tillich pretended to teach the Christian doctrine of God but in actuality was putting forward a concept of God quite different from that of the "orthodox" Christian tradition. In particular, the accusation maintained, Tillich's view of God was not at all the same as the teaching about God to be found in the great Christian theologian of the fifth century, Augustine of Hippo.

Apart from what one's evaluation of Tillich's theology might be, the accusation discloses an interesting perspective and an important problem. A central presupposition underlying the attack appears to be that theology cannot change because religion either does not change or ought not change. Religion is defined by an orthodoxy, itself based on the doctrine of some particular time in the past. And apparently, religion cannot change because it believes in a static deity enshrined in that orthodoxy. If theology does change, according to Tillich's accuser, the shift is clear evidence that the religious tradition of the past is being betrayed.

As we have already seen, no historical, theological, or sociological investigation of religion can sustain the view that religion is a static, unchanging phenomenon. In the same way, theology wrestling in faith with ultimate issues cannot remain fixed. Theology is undergoing constant change. Indeed, if Paul Tillich had been only repeating fifth-century theological formulations, as his critic apparently expected him to do, then Tillich would have been betraying the great Augustine of Hippo.

Few thinkers in the entire history of human believing offer clearer examples of change as a theological occurrence than does Augustine. He pulled together many lines of theological thought that had been developing as the Christian movement encountered the religious and philosophical diversity of the Roman Empire. In the process, he performed a massive and epoch-making reinterpretation of Christian theology. Far from reinforcing stasis in theology, Augustine led a major transformation of Christian theology, solidified the shape of a new theological paradigm, and provided a powerful witness to Christian faith that continued into the Middle Ages, into the time of the Reformation, and into our own century to influence theological reflection.

In spite of clear evidence of change in views of deity, a widespread though not universal postulate of the Western intellectual tradition has been that ultimate reality is changeless. This notion can be traced back to the sources of Western thought in early Hellenic philosophy. Francis Cornford suggests that this philosophical assumption is rooted in early Greek religion, in which the dynamism of the gods is subordinate to a static order known as Destiny or *Moira*. Cornford writes:

The philosophic Muse is not a motherless Athena: if the individual intellect is her father, her older and more august parent is Religion. . . . A real thread of continuity can be traced back from the final achievement of science—the representation of a world of individual atoms, governed by Necessity or Chance—to the final achievement of Olympianism, mirrored in Homer's supernatural world of individual Gods, subordinate to Destiny *(Moira)* . . . which . . . holds the place now occupied by Natural Law.[6]

Greek thought cannot, of course, be regarded as monolithic on this issue. Parmenides argues from the presupposition of static Being and asserts that only Being—what is—can be thought; whereas Not Being—what is not—cannot be thought. With that presupposition and Parmenides' logical rigor, change could not be thought. By contrast, Heraclitus teaches that the unity of opposites is the basis of reality and, therefore, "we step and we do no step into the same river." Plato sought to combine the rigor of Parmenides with the inclusiveness of Heraclitus. He overcame Parmenides' rejection of Not Being by showing it has at least two meanings: (1) that which *is not,* in the sense of partaking in no way of Being; or (2) that which *is not* in the sense that a bird is not a fish or a boy not yet a man. Not being becomes the basis for distinguishing the variety of human experiencing. In the Platonic dialectic, all that can be said to be partakes of Being and Becoming, of continuity and change. An irreducible mark of Being is power, *dynamis* (*Sophist,* 247E).

In contrast to the restless reality of Plato, Aristotle combined all that was immutable into the Unmoved Mover and left all change in the subordinate movement from potentiality to actuality within the ultimate reality of God. It is this notion of static deity, filtered through the Neoplatonism of Plotinus, which provides the philosophic setting of the Christian theology of Augustine. Aristotle's strong influence on medieval theology is transferred directly through the thought of Thomas Aquinas.

The Aristotelian view of ultimate reality as static stands in strange contrast to the biblical view of an unknown, restless Yahweh. Moses asks for God's name to use when he comes to the people of Israel. "God said to Moses, 'I am who I am. . . . Say this to the People of Israel, "I am has sent me to you" ' " (Exod. 3:14). We must remember that the name might be translated "I will be what I will be." Form and continuity derive from God's covenant faithfulness, not from a static nature. Thus the antithesis between dynamism and stasis is overcome in the faithful will of the final power of nature and history. But this view has not been dominant. A. O. Lovejoy states the puzzle of Western theology:

It is true that the God of Aristotle had almost nothing in common with the God of the Sermon on the Mount—though, by one of the strangest and most monstrous paradoxes in Western history, the philosophical theology of Christendom identified them, and defined the chief end of man as the imitation of both. But it is also true that Aristotle's conception of the being to whom he gave the most honorific name he knew was merely a consequence of a certain more general way of thinking, a species of dialectic . . . not peculiar to him but highly characteristic of the Greek and almost wholly foreign to the ancient Jewish Mind.[7]

RELIGION AND CHANGE

Though never without dissenting alternatives, the dominant view in the Constantinian paradigm of Western theology, in Western philosophy, and in Western science has been the notion of a static reality underlying all change. The extreme statement of this view is a Laplacean physical atomism in which change, diversity, and time are explained as shifting configurations of particles according to immutable laws. Laplace affirms change only within a static order of determinism.

The static view of deity and reality has come under increasing question from various directions: from the covenant theology which emerged from the biblical studies of the Reformation, from Hegel and Marx, from Kierkegaard and the existentialists, from the process philosophers, by the emergence of relativity theory and the principles of complementarity and uncertainty in the physical sciences, and from the impetus toward liberation of the past century.

It is doubtful that theology can operate with a notion of absolute flux as ultimate reality. Nevertheless, the shift away from static notions of deity and reality is important for contemporary Christian theology. This becomes clear as we consider how theology can deal with the challenges of pluralism and liberation. For example, theological change can refer only to societal change or to change in human believing so long as the deity or reality in which humans believe is conceived to be static. This view can handle the evolution of a particular religious tradition, but not the changes that result when different traditions meet or when the drive toward human liberation breaks out of repressive theological structures. We must seek new ways to relate deity and change.

Some traditions of faith, including the biblical faith in Yahweh, regard reality or deity more as a moving target for human believing than as a fixed object. God in biblical perspective is the Faithful One—reliable but not static—whose covenantal action includes past, present, *and* future. In this view, theological change can work with the varied and changing patterns of faith—to explore them in themselves as well as to appraise their bearing on reality. The relation of deity and change can be viewed in at least four ways: (1) in terms of the relativity of human location and the resulting partial, changing perspectives on deity; (2) in terms of methodological complementarity between stasis and dynamism, with neither seen as adequate alone to describe ultimate reality; (3) as a mystery to be understood in part in terms of an uncertainty principle; or (4) as it is understood here, the reality of the covenant God, faithfully in process toward a redeeming, liberating consummation hidden in the future.

Many continue to look to religion to provide a static basis of security in a changing world. Their search seems doomed to disappointment. There appears to be no protected homeland; the religion of the past is indeed dissolving; religious dogmas cannot make the world stand still. Religious faith, viewed historically and cross-culturally, testifies to human believing as a changing phenomenon. Theology and ethics must be transformed in method so that they may deal with the levels of change in society, change in religious faith, and change in relation to deity. Only then will theology point to possibilities of discovering our homeland in the human journey on the way of liberation.

We have suggested a new vision of the problem of religion and change. In this perspective religion is neither a static entity nor absolute flux. Religious believing serves to orient humans within change. Human believing fulfills its purpose only through being taken up anew in unanticipated ways in every generation. Continuity with the past as well as change are inevitable components of human believing in each new era. In this perspective, we can anticipate the changing of the gods. But this does not mean theological catastrophe. Rather it is the way human communities *dwell in* their faith in order to *break out* toward God's future. The absorption of change is always a central purpose of religion; and this purpose of religion means ever new beginnings. For

Christian faith, and perhaps for other faiths as well, the continuing absorption of change enables us to perceive the action of the covenant God, ever new, ever faithful, whose power can be traced in the saving history of liberation.

VIII.

THE MEANING OF THEOLOGICAL TRANSFORMATION

Religion and change are not antithetical; in the realm of human believing, they complement and complete one another. Change applies also, as we have seen, to believed-in gods and therefore must be regarded as a theological phenomenon.

It is one thing to say that change is something for theology to note, consider, and utilize. It is quite another to say that theology itself must change. But that is exactly what I have been suggesting. Now we shall take a further step and examine more carefully what it means to speak of theological transformation.

First of all, is fundamental change in theology possible? The answer, as I see it, must be an unequivocal affirmative. Theological reflection evolves and revises its method, style, and content in response to alterations in believed-in deities and in response to changes in socio-cultural conditions. The human story—whether from Egypt or Mesopotamia, from Hellas or Rome, from India or Japan, from America or Russia—is replete with examples of shifts in patterns of human action and commitment. As reflection on and articulation of the ultimate dimensions of the commitments governing action, theology cannot avoid undergoing change. If religion serves its purpose by continual change, then theology can fulfill itself only through transformation. Indeed, it is by means of transformation that theology is able to come to grips with changing configurations of culture and faith.

Second, even though it is possible, will Western theology undergo transformation? This is a more difficult question, though I have stated my own conviction that the process of change is already clearly visible. Resistance is strong and will continue. The Constantinian paradigm that has governed Western theology for over a millennium has become so entrenched that it is difficult for conventional theologians to conceive of theological change, much less to imagine a shape for theology other than the familiar one. Shifting cultural conditions are creating tensions, however, that can no longer be resisted. As with a fault in the earth, the shifting land masses build up increasing pressure. If there are no small temblors to adjust the segments to one another, the result eventually will be a major earthquake. Something of this nature has been occurring in the shifting sectors of human believing. As the tension between the traditional paradigm and the changing religio-cultural situation has increased, a self-confident and assured theology of the North Atlantic academies has ignored the shifting landscape and resisted change. As a result, the process of theological transformation away from Constantinian patterns is more traumatic than it might have been otherwise.

Third, how are we to understand theological transformation? That is the central question addressed in this chapter. The answer to the first question seems clear. The answer to the second will find its answer as events unfold. This third question requires more careful exploration than it has been given so far. Because alterations in patterns of faith have to do with changes in the comprehensive shape of human action and commitment, religious and theological change is more easily discerned at a distance. This may be distance in time, as with religious changes in the Roman Empire perceived from the twentieth century, or cultural distance, as with patterns of faith and thought in Burma seen from America, or distance of noninvolvement, as with stories in the press about the children of other parents joining a cult. Until we understand better the meaning of theological transformation, we shall not be equipped to perceive and deal with the changing configurations of commitment and action taking place around us, in our own traditions, in our own society, in our own lives.

1. The Point of Departure

Lost in a rural area where signposts were either absent or illegible, ambiguous or misleading, a confused tourist stopped his car and asked a farmer the way to his destination. The farmer scratched his grizzled beard thoughtfully, looked first in one direction along the sandy road and then in the other. At last, he turned to the waiting traveler and replied, "I'll tell ya, stranger, if I was going *there,* I wouldn't start from *here.*"

The response is especially instructive for coming to understand religious faith and theology in a time such as ours. There are locations which assure that the gods remain invisible and from which it is therefore unwise to begin if we wish to see the scene of human believing and discover the meaning of theological transformation.

Certain points of departure make it impossible to deal with religious commitments because of limiting postulates or philosophical "catch 22s." It is as though we were sorting pieces of cloth and, after discarding all those over three inches in length, complained that cloth came only in short lengths; or, after baking a batch of cookies using only one cookie cutter, we announced that cookies always come in a single shape. "All Indians walk in single file," concluded the empirical researcher, "at least, the one I saw did." Points of departure involving conceptual limitations can severely restrict our ability to deal with the varieties of human experiencing. And nowhere is this lesson more apparent than with reference to the patterns governing religious studies and theology.

For example, the presupposition that religious belief is superstition is one point of departure that I do not recommend. Another is that all religiosity is based on illusion. Though one might come to these conclusions, they are scarcely helpful places to begin if one wishes to understand the meaning of faith for those who believe or to discover the relation of conviction to action. "When you do not hear the music, the dancers seem mad." So it is with all understandings of religion that eliminate its meaning in advance.

A third view of religion, which does not offer a helpful point of departure in the present situation, is the limitation of religious significance to a single ecclesiastical community. This leads to what I have called ecclesiastical theology, the conventional pattern of Western theology. We have had occasion to suggest how the fortuitous triumph of the Judeo-Christian faith led to the conceptual reduction of religion to this single form and to the resultant limitation of European theology. Adherents of other faiths were excluded from attention as unbelievers and infidels; what they believed was rendered theologically meaningless. Other religions, other gods became invisible. And this limitation led, in the period of sectarian strife, to the further reduction of religious and theological meaning to the property of a single enclave. Such a narrow point of departure is of limited usefulness, given the global configuration of pluralism and liberation.

A fourth unhappy point of departure combines one or another of the above perspectives with the traditional bifurcations of the Western philosophy. The problems of dealing with the contemporary religious situation are then compounded. Religious believing becomes restricted to one side or the other of a dichotomized world. Either it is objective and therefore to be verified, or subjective and existentialized.

When religion becomes an objectivized reality, theology deals with the faith even of a single community only in terms of the settled past. Comprehending the changing present, as that community evolves and relates to other communities, is beyond the conceptual capabilities of a theology in which religion has been reduced to institutional stasis. In this view, tradition is not so much an ordered flow of change as the reification of a particular era. Orthodoxy tends to be regarded as the religion enshrined in the faith of some prior generation. The symbiosis of believing and communal experiencing goes unperceived, as religion becomes a static entity which is judged by the present as receding. Reified religion always appears to be declining. Yet mysteriously it never disappears. Human believing as it changes with historical circumstances is neither recognized nor charted by theology.

Such an "objective" view of religion has not been restricted to theology. It has flowed into and been utilized by sectors of religious studies and social science. Reified religion can be studied empirically. Its members can be counted, in Western society at least. Attendance at services, financial data, building, institutional organization, class and status information on participants, responses to questions about theological and social opinions can be studied, tabulated on computers, and reported.

This notion of religion fits nicely into the phenomenal, scientific sector of Kant's bifurcated world. Any reference to believed-in reality can be discounted or ignored in this empirical approach. The "facts" will suffice. It is not surprising that a sociology or theology based upon such conceptualization confronts major difficulties as the pluralism of religious consciousness has emerged into view and the thrust toward human liberation has become a primary factor in global culture.

On the other hand, given a bifurcated world, religion can be reduced to a "subjective" reality. Here religious believing is understood existentially. Faith becomes all-important. God cannot be apprehended by means of objective categories but only through human subjectivity.

THE MEANING OF THEOLOGICAL TRANSFORMATION

The historical and societal dimensions of faith may be rejected so totally that faith and religion come to be regarded as antithetical. Faith has to do only with self-understanding and the future, not with understanding of the past or understanding of society and the cosmos. Science deals with the objective and cannot endanger faith which is subjective. And so we swing from one side of the traditional dichotomy to the other, from the phenomenal to the noumenal, from the theoretic to the practical, from the objective to the subjective—and then back again.

We must be careful about our point of departure. Happily we are not limited to those places to begin described above. There is another location that has been taking shape and acquiring an increasing number of adherents.

One source of this different perspective is to be found in the recovery of biblical perspectives on human life. Another source is the stream of covenant theology that flows from Heinrich Bullinger, finds its fullest expression in Johannes Cocceius, and merges into process thought and into the federal societal patterns of global society. Still other resources are to be found in the daring and difficult work of Charles Sanders Peirce and the innovative physical theories of Willard Gibbs. The genius of William James lifted Peirce's insights from their obscure setting, gave them brilliant expression, and provided the inspiration for some of the most important movements of thought in the twentieth century. Such diverse figures as Josiah Royce, John Dewey, Max Weber, Ernst Troeltsch, and Edmund Husserl were influenced by James. Stream-of-consciousness literature and Gestalt psychology find in him a mentor. George Herbert Mead and Harry Stack Sullivan must be counted among his intellectual progeny. And the directions of thought fostered by Peirce and James find rich and original expression in Michael Polanyi and H. Richard Niebuhr.

These sources have already informed the description of the mystery of human location (chapter 5) and the understanding of the symbiotic relation of religion and change (chapter 7). Now my point of departure will be made more explicit. It is crucial, I am convinced, to begin, not with the ecclesiastical limitations and philosophical bifurcations of the Constantinian paradigm, but rather with the covenantal wholeness of human experiencing.

2. Covenantal Wholeness

Though I do not intend to "disprove" or "falsify" the assumptions that would limit theology to ecclesiastical premises or the presuppositions of ontological/epistemological bifurcation, I no longer find them appropriate for theological reflection. It is not that I have achieved a superior vantage point for surveying reality and think that I can "prove" or "verify" my perspective. I speak from human location and perspective. I can, however, explain the reasons the shift appears to be important. From the human perspective that I occupy, I no longer find the presuppositional field of the Constantinian paradigm persuasive. The limitation to ecclesiastical spheres cuts theology off from pluralism in its inclusive dimensions and therefore prevents precision in dealing with the varied texture of believing in Western society and in the emerging global culture. The same limitations, viewed in political-economic perspective, tend to cut theology and theologians off from movements of liberation, as important in global culture as pluralism. On the level of basic concepts, the split world of the traditional paradigm segregates religion and God into special sectors of experience. Religious faith and believed-in gods have meaning only in relation to the wholeness of experiencing, a wholeness given shape by the covenants of human living.

The shift of postulates I propose may be illumined by comparing it with the change that has occurred in geometry. Euclidean axioms and postulates have not been rejected as false. They still are considered as providing a presuppositional field appropriate for limited situations involving simple planes. But Euclidean assumptions are not adequate for dealing with astral distances and infinite space-time. For this expanded situation, one must start from a different location. It is for similar reasons that a different point of departure, a different presuppositional location, is needed if theology is to cope with an expanded and expanding cultural situation.

What I am proposing here for theology may most accurately be called a covenantal or federal paradigm. Some understanding of this pattern has already been suggested in earlier chapters. In this section, I shall specify the point of departure for this paradigm in the wholeness of human experiencing. In subsequent sections, we shall be filling in further elements comprising this paradigm and its theological method.

Ecclesiastical limits and intellectual bifurcations of experience are not adequate for dealing with the ultimate commitments informing human action and the believed-in realities providing the focus of religious faith. Indeed, these traditional presuppositions are impediments when we set out to explore encompassing meanings of selves in community. Theology must widen its scope and deal with the varieties of faith as they appear in the experienced wholeness of individuals and communities, not as empirical particulars limited to special sectors of experience.

With reference to the traditional dichotomies of European philosophy, there seems to be no basis for assuming splits in a human experiencing present to us only in unbroken wholeness. Quite clearly, differentiations within this wholeness are possible and appropriate. Yet the primary apprehension of reality is of a totality. Our experiencing emerges from a primal wholeness which is constantly changing yet manifesting patterns of increasing variety and complexity, continually expanding in scope and inclusiveness.

Similarly, there is no basis for assuming the strange

bifurcation between "Being" and "appearance," with its variants "substance" and "accident," "noumenon" and "phenomenon," "reality" and "experience," "objective" and "subjective." How can we speak of any one of these separated from its counterpart? It would appear possible to speak of Being only in terms of what appears. If it does not appear in some manner, then it has for us no location, no being. On the other hand, whatever appears may be said *to be* in some sense and can be assigned location within the totality that we believe our world to be. By mode and pattern of relation, we distinguish and locate what appears within a comprehensive wholeness.

The wholeness of experiencing as embodied in commitment and action are shaped by religious faith and God. Diverse religions, gods, and faith-perspectives appear in the differing patterns of human worlds. Changing gods and faiths occur in the shifting shapes, in the reordering of commitments and actions, of wholes. This ordering of priorities in action means that valuing permeates the wholeness of experiencing. The pattern of experience involves axiological location no less than ontological relation. It is to this ontological-axiological shape that we refer when we speak of religious faith and gods in human communities; we are not referring to some imagined world that in some unspecified and unspecifiable way is "behind," "above," or "beneath" what appears.

William James stands among the most striking and influential figures who questioned the bifurcation and fragmentation assumed in European thought and proposed to start from the wholeness of experience. In his opposition to associationism in psychology, James demonstrates that he is a forerunner of Gestalt psychology. His thought anticipates and is a prime factor in developing the social psychology that emphasizes the interpretation of social and individual factors in the wholeness of experiencing. This wholeness James articulated as stream of consciousness, which implied his emphatic rejection of experiential atomism. One commentator, Margaret

Knight, writes: "As James pointed out, though it may
sometimes be convenient to treat experience as consisting
of separate ideas and sensations (just as it is convenient
for certain purposes to treat a line as a series of points, or
a river as a collection of drops), these divisions do not
really exist in nature. They are 'mere arbitrary results of
conceptual handling on our part.' "[1]

James helped to initiate a revolution in our thinking
about human experiencing that leads toward understanding our world in its wholeness rather than as
bifurcated, in continuity rather than as fragmented. He
emphasizes in his *Principles of Psychology:* first, that
consciousness is continuous, a seamless whole; second,
that it includes not entities so much as relations and
transitions; and, third, that it has a fringe as well as a
focus. "Though attention is focused on a centre," Knight
continues,

we are always aware of a vague and sliding stream of
impressions and sensations at the periphery. The limitations of
language make it difficult to give facts of this kind their due
weight in describing our mental life; but James was peculiarly
fitted to deal with this difficulty, since he had an exceptional
power of fixing and crystallizing the most elusive and fugitive
states of consciousness; as Perry says, "he could see most
cunningly out of the corners of his eyes." His genius is
demonstrated, for example, in his account of the experience of
searching one's memory for a forgotten fact and in his
description of the "revelatory experience" as he comes to from
nitrous oxide. These illustrations show how successfully he
fulfilled his declared intention of "reinstating the vague and
inarticulate to its proper place in our mental life."[2]

Building upon the insights of James, Gestalt psychology has done much to provide ways of speaking of the
wholeness of experiencing and thus to make the
traditional bifurcations less persuasive. In philosophy,
Edmund Husserl, Alfred North Whitehead, and Gilbert
Ryle have, in diverse ways, been effective critics of these
divisions. Michael Polanyi[3] has, I believe, produced the

most convincing account of knowing that does not rely on the usual dichotomies. In so doing he has inaugurated the post-critical era of Western thought.

By taking as our point of departure the wholeness of human experiencing,[4] we avoid conceptual reductions of religion. First, theology is enabled to take account of faiths beyond that of a particular community, not to eliminate particularity, but rather to be aware of the believing and valuing present in the experiencing and acting of all humans. Theology is then no longer limited to particular ecclesiastical enclaves, though the problem of the particular commitments and presuppositions of the theologian in relation to alternative perspectives is not overcome. Second, this point of departure avoids the conceptual reduction of religion to a particular sector of human experience. Theology directs itself toward the wholeness and the comprehensive rather than toward the objective, the subjective, or some other sector defined by the bifurcations of the Western philosophical tradition.

When we begin, not with bifurcations and disjunctions, but with experienced wholeness, two aspects of this wholeness come into view. First, wholeness is present to us in community. As we shall see in chapter 9, this view requires a triadic view of knowing, with social and historical dimensions, in contrast to the dyadic epistemology of most Western thought, with the knower-known relation identified with the subject-object dyad. And second, it is covenantal wholeness, made up of commitments, loyalty, and faith. It is in interaction with others that we internalize the fabric of this wholeness and learn to articulate its components. As we come to share and affirm the particular commitments and loyalties that bind our own experiencing together, this wholeness takes on reality and valency for us.

Religious change refers to a basic shift in the pattern of commitments pervading the wholeness of experiencing shared by persons in community. Theological transformation refers to a fundamental change in the concepts and methods by which theologians understand and describe human believing and its gods. But theologians are also religious and work within, not above and beyond, the particular wholeness of experience belonging to their own community and covenants. Given this situation, how can we distinguish theological transformation that participates in religious faith but is not identical with it?

3. Paradigms in Crisis and Change

To clarify further the meaning of theological transformation, we must distinguish different levels of comprehensiveness in the covenantal wholeness of human experiencing. When these levels are not distinguished we fall into what Gilbert Ryle calls a category mistake. This error involves confusing different levels of comprehensiveness. To illustrate his point Ryle tells several stories.

A foreigner visiting Oxford or Cambridge for the first time is shown a number of colleges, libraries, playing fields, museums, scientific departments and administrative offices. He then asks "But where is the University? I have seen where the members of the Colleges live, where the Registrar works, where the scientists experiment and the rest. But I have not yet seen the University in which reside and work the members of your University." It has then to be explained to him that the University is not another collateral institution. . . . The University is just the way in which all that he has already seen is organized. . . . His mistake lay in his innocent assumption that it was correct to speak of Christ Church, the Bodleian Library, the Ashmolean Museum *and* the University, to speak, that is, as if "the University" stood for an extra member of the class of which these other units are members. He was mistakenly allocating the University to the same category as that to which the other institutions belong.[5]

Another example of a category mistake given by Ryle involves a person watching a division of troops march past. After having battalions, batteries, and squadrons pointed out to him, he might ask when the division would appear. His category mistake would be shown by telling him "that in watching the battalions, batteries and squadrons marching past he had been watching the division marching past. The march-past was not a parade of battalions, batteries, squadrons *and* a division; it was a parade of the battalions, batteries and squadrons *of* a division."[6] In similar fashion someone might wonder that the forwards, guards, and center of a basketball team leave no player to provide team spirit. The category mistake is made in expecting team spirit to be a separable operation rather than a function of the entire team in its playing.

In a similar way, it is a category mistake to look for human religiousness in a sector of life rather than in the whole of living. Let us designate this most inclusive wholeness of human acting, intending, and believing a "realm of actuality."[7] Whether referring to individuals or communities, religiousness pertains to a realm of actuality. A person may go to church on Sunday or engage in devotional exercises at a particular time each day. But it is a category mistake to reduce a person's or a group's religious faith to what occurs at only one time. Religious faith is that which pervades a realm of actuality. A god is that reality believed in as shaping history and our realm of actuality.

Thomas Kuhn, a historian of science, suggests a way to understand the patterns scholars use to deal with their subjects and the ways these patterns change. His analysis refers to transformations in method and conceptualization within the community of the natural scientists. Kuhn's work is based to a considerable degree on the thought of Peirce and Gibbs, and especially on Michael Polanyi's philosophy. His book, *The Structure of Scientific Revolutions,* is imaginatively conceived, throws light on the development of the natural sciences, and does much to shatter positivistic notions about scientific methodology and insight. With modification, what he says can also be utilized, I am convinced, to illumine what is occurring in theological method today, as it wrestles with pluralism and liberation.

Kuhn speaks of successive periods in the development of science as being distinguished by their different relations to what Kuhn calls paradigms. In a "normal" phase of the history of science, a scientific community operates on shared assumptions and works out the implications of this stable view. "Men whose research is based on shared paradigms," he asserts, "are committed to the same rules and standards for scientific practice. That commitment and the apparent consensus it produces are prerequisites for normal science, *i.e.,* for the genesis and continuation of a particular research tradition." In a "revolutionary" phase of the history of science, the dominance of the reigning paradigm is questioned, comes into crisis, is discarded, and is replaced by another paradigm. The new paradigm then shapes the work of the next era of science. Kuhn calls the shift from one paradigm to another a scientific revolution. "After a revolution," writes Kuhn, "scientists are responding to a different world."[8]

The most dramatic illustrations of scientific revolutions appear in the change from the Ptolemaic paradigm to the Copernican one and in the shift from the Newtonian to the Einsteinian paradigm. But Kuhn refers also to less well-known transitions in the basic concepts and methods governing parts of the scientific community.

What is a paradigm? At one point, Kuhn describes a paradigm as comprising a "strong network of commitments —conceptual, theoretical, instrumental, and methodological"—which "is the principal source of the metaphor that relates normal science to puzzle-solving"[9] in a specific movement or era. In the second edition of his book Kuhn writes of a paradigm:

On the one hand, it stands for the entire constellation of beliefs, values, techniques, and so on, shared by members of a given community. On the other hand, it denotes one sort of element in that constellation, the concrete puzzle-solutions which, employed as models or examples, can replace explicit rules as a basis for the solution of the remaining puzzles of normal science.[10]

As an era of normal science comes to a close, the dominance of the paradigm begins to weaken within the community controlled by it. Problems from the paradigm no longer seem so interesting or fruitful as earlier. Anomalies, data that cannot be fitted into the paradigm, appear; inadequacies in the paradigm develop; it is no longer possible to ignore or reinterpret data that the paradigm will not encompass. Dissatisfaction with the prevailing paradigm arises, and probing for a new paradigm emerges. The aging paradigm is in crisis.

New presuppositions and perspectives begin to be explored. Attempts at a different integration of information occur. These probes are not so much taking account of new data as seeking for a new way to look at what is already known. Intuitive visions elaborating new paradigms arise. One of these may appeal so strongly to the scientific community in which it appears that it leads to the discarding of the paradigm that is in crisis and the adoption of the new paradigm. With the change, new possibilities are seen; new patterns emerge; new problems, some foreseen, others unsuspected, develop. A new era of normal science within the new paradigm is under way.

The pattern that Kuhn suggests may be utilized for understanding change in theology. In a fashion parallel to Kuhn's scientific revolutions, we may speak of theological transformation as the change from one paradigm to another. One era of theology is characterized by a strong network of commitments—conceptual, theoretical, methodological, and instrumental; theologians of that era pursue solutions to the problems present within this controlling paradigm. In the paradigmatic frame an era of "normal theology" takes place, and its particular puzzles emerge and are unraveled. Then anomalies begin to appear. Data that once gave no difficulty are no longer seen as fitting into the paradigm. Sectors of experience, once excluded or ignored as irrelevant, now seem too important to be omitted; the paradigm is not adequate to encompass these areas.

Increasingly, the problems of this "normal theology" are less interesting than those posed by the presence of the anomalous data. Probing around and beyond the prevailing conceptual frame occurs. In these ways, that paradigm and the normal theology defined by it come into crisis. As the crisis develops, turmoil and uncertainty disrupt the prevailing patterns of theology. In the midst of the confusion, attempts at reformulation, thrusts toward possible new paradigms, appear. One of these intuitive visions may emerge into dominance, be elaborated into a conceptual frame and methodology and become the controlling paradigm for a new era of normal theology. This is what a theological transformation would look like if we apply Kuhn's notion of a scientific revolution.

From the perspective suggested by Kuhn, we have been witnessing the end of the era of normal theology governed by the Constantinian paradigm. The global culture emerging today cannot be understood within the limited conceptual frame of ecclesiastical theology and a bifurcated world. If the theological systems of the past seem dated and material only for doctoral dissertations, if turmoil in theology is more apparent than stability, it may not be total confusion but rather the restless probing toward a new paradigm. New theological theory, concepts, and methods are needed if we are to make sense of the confrontation now in process on a global scale among multiple life-styles and faith-perspectives competing for power to shape the future.

The revolution in religious thought now under way brings into crisis the Constantinian paradigm, which has governed conventional theology in the West since the time of Augustine.[11] The present crisis involves a breaking out toward a new pattern appropriate for a theology able to deal with pluralism and liberation in the emerging global culture.

Kuhn's notion of paradigm enables us to see the pattern by which scholarly communities work and to understand the changes that take place in the network of commitments governing the operation of these communities. With the perspective drawn from Kuhn, a meaning for theological transformation emerges, a meaning that distinguishes theological change from religious change yet illumines the close relation between them. In addition, the stresses and strains upon the inherited theological paradigm, causing the extreme dis-ease in contemporary theology, become intelligible. The crisis, heralding a breaking-out of one paradigm and the formation of another, rather than being obscured by the turmoil, now becomes available for examination. Theology as practiced in the Western world exists between one era now drawing to a close and another just dawning. A profound transformation in theology is taking place around us.

To glimpse the meaning of theological change, however, is only a beginning. We must explore the direction of movement, investigate theoretical and conceptual changes involved in this transformation, and seek with all our power of imagination to envisage a shape for the theology of the future. This task requires extending the meaning of paradigm beyond that intended by Kuhn and drawing on resources wider than those used by him.

As we begin to delineate a new paradigm for a transformed theology, it is important to remember that, as has already been emphasized, the crucial context is pluralism. But the means for understanding the power of religious change lies in the notion of liberation. One who sees the issue clearly and states it directly is Benjamin Reist.

The struggle for liberation from ethnic oppression has forced the oppressed/oppressor dialectic into the open at the level of primary consideration. It cannot be treated as if the object were simply to gain new insights for incorporation into a theological apparatus assumed to be basically sound already. The transformation of the entire style of theological reflection is involved.[12]

THE MEANING OF THEOLOGICAL TRANSFORMATION

As theological change occurs in response to the significant and far-reaching changes taking place in the religious situation of humanity, the struggle against oppression moves to the fore. The decisive key to a paradigm adequate for a transformed theology is liberation.

PART THREE

METHOD: COVENANT AND LIBERATION

All that has gone before, the strivings of a myriad centres that have taken the risks of living and believing, seem to have all been pursuing . . . the aim now achieved by us up to this point . . . . For all these centres—those which led up to our own existence and the far more numerous others which produced different lines of which many are extinct—may be seen engaged in the same endeavor *towards ultimate liberation* . . . towards an unthinkable consummation.

Michael Polanyi

We are concerned now with faith as dependence on a value-center and as loyalty to a cause. Hence when we speak of "gods" we mean the gods of faith, namely, such value-centers and causes.

H. Richard Niebuhr

IX.

A FEDERAL PARADIGM

At an Orthodox Jewish synagogue recently, while
attending a Bar Mitzvah, I had time during the
three-hour service, all in Hebrew, for reflection on the
power of story and ritual to shape our lives. Yarmulke on
my head, seated on the all-male side of the congregation,
my Hebrew not good enough to follow the service with
ease, I spent the time absorbing the atmosphere and
observing my fellow worshipers. There were the formal
elements—readings from the prayer book; bringing out
the Torah, carrying it around the entire synagogue,
reading at length from it, male members of the
congregation taking turns, and then the ritual of taking it
back to its place of honor. The informal elements
combined with these to give an atmosphere of intense
participation. Several worshipers engaged in a distinctive
rocking motion from one foot to the other during the
readings, as though reliving some deep sorrow. A few
used their prayer shawls as head covering, as though for
private grief. There was the magnificent rhythm of the
hymns, the moving story of exodus and liberation
coursing through the Torah readings.

As I participated, a community of interpretation and
faith became visible around me, a community with deep
roots in the past and profoundly serious involvement in

the present. Over there I noted the author of a new book on business ethics, to my left a respected civic leader, ahead a prominent political scientist, behind me a world-famous scholar of rabbinic Judaism, and, beyond the fence separating men and women, a woman who had just completed her doctorate in history. Here were real people, with the wholeness of their experiencing shaped by this worship, its story giving them meaning and a history. They dwell in a world similar to mine, yet very different. The biblical story gives us a common context for understanding what is valuable and worth doing. At the same time, the exclusion of women from leadership and the segregation by sex reminded my wife and me that our lives are informed by other patterns of meaning. I found the partial participation and the continuing distance instructive. Can we develop theological methods for understanding the varied worlds of human believing, even as we remain aware that we dwell in one of them rather than soaring to a perspective above them all?

We have made a beginning. We have looked at the context requiring theological change and at a perspective for understanding theological transformation. Now we are ready to explore a method for theology in a global culture of pluralism and liberation. This task will be accomplished (1) by describing the basic components of a federal or covenantal paradigm; (2) by providing reconceptualized understandings of God and religion; and (3) by showing the symbiotic relation between pluralism and liberation in a transformed theology.

Underlying the analysis in the previous chapters has been a new paradigm for theology. Because the root metaphor of this paradigm is covenant, it can most accurately be called a federal paradigm. The words federal and federalism derive from the Latin *foedus*, which means covenant. A federal paradigm for theology or political philosophy is at its core covenantal, though political scientists and historians as well as theologians have often forgotten the relation. The new paradigm can, therefore, be given the alternative name covenantal.

The clue to historical direction and purpose in the federal paradigm is to be found in liberation. For Christian faith, liberation characterizes the faithful action of God recounted in Scripture and revealed in Jesus Christ. The historical and natural orders are filled with the creative, judging, liberating governance of the Faithful One. This perspective should not be construed, however, as providing Christians with a transhistorical viewpoint by means of which to dehistorize history and eliminate the mystery of God's future. The pluralistic faiths around the globe and the surges of oppressed peoples in all cultures toward liberation dissolve the limited conceptions of God, Jesus Christ, and history transmitted to us by our Christian past and open us to widened perspectives and an emerging consummation hidden in God. As theological principle, liberation is, therefore, both historical catalyst and solvent.

In order to explain the meaning of a federal pattern for theology, we must extend Kuhn's notion of paradigm. The first extension involves interpreting paradigm in terms of the covenants that shape human living. The second extension requires going behind Thomas Kuhn's thought to that of Michael Polanyi, and drawing on this seminal thinker for an understanding of the communal basis of human commitment and the tacit dimension underlying knowing and acting. The third extension involves utilizing the notion of liberation, not only as future hope but also as a present dwelling in and breaking out, by means of which continuity and change are related to the sovereign reality of history and nature. In this way, we shall develop a federal paradigm for theology.

On the one hand, a federal paradigm has a biblical provenance. By drawing on the Bible and its treatment of covenant, I shall evoke the resources of the Judeo-Christian tradition in all its prophetic power to address the meaning of justice and liberation for the contemporary global situation. Any theology that does not understand and work to overcome oppressions of all kinds is unworthy of the biblical heritage.

A FEDERAL PARADIGM

On the other hand, the federal perspective opens the way to understanding the nature of human existence in community. It directs attention to those primal covenants and consciousness in which societies, from the most primitive to the most developed, are rooted. By restoring the close connection between covenant and federalism, we can see once again the political and societal forms embodying cultural diversity and nurturing both pluralism and liberation in Western society. A federal paradigm enables theology to penetrate the wholeness of human experiencing, to appreciate its variety, to perceive the religious significance of shifting patterns of commitment, and to comprehend the meaning of pluralism and change for human liberation.

1. Covenants of Human Living

Thomas Kuhn speaks of a paradigm as the "strong network of commitments—conceptual, theoretical, instrumental, and methodological"—that guides a scientific community in its investigations and is "a principal source of the metaphor that relates normal science to puzzle-solving."[1] In this use of paradigm, Kuhn is already going beyond its ordinary meaning as pattern, example, or model. I believe that the meaning can be extended even further.

By referring to a paradigm as a strong network of commitments, Kuhn indicates the covenantal character of research communities and suggests levels of commitments governing thinking and action in these communities. The paradigm, understood as a field with levels of increasing valency, may also be understood as comprehended in a controlling metaphor. Extended to include in the network a level of religious commitment pervading the whole and strengthened by use of the term "root metaphor"[2] for the governing image, Kuhn's paradigm becomes a federal paradigm relating the most comprehensive horizons of believed-in reality, the intermediate purposes and values directing action, and the everyday concepts, instrumentalities, and activities of human living.

The federal paradigm, understood in this way, is intended to be applicable in two ways important for a transformed theology. First, it enables us to understand the network of commitments informing a community of theological inquiry as it explores the religious meaning of human experiencing. In extended form, Kuhn's paradigm seems no less applicable to theological than to scientific investigation. I have spoken already in this way of the Constantinian paradigm governing theological inquiry in the Western tradition and its crisis and dissolution in the twentieth century. Second, the federal paradigm enables us to understand the wholeness of human experiencing as a network of commitments, as a field of believing and valuing. This opens the way for theological and ethical inquiry so that the investigators can deal with their own locations in communities of faith and interpretation yet can also explore the diverse communities and faith-perspectives around them. The federal paradigm aids in coping both with pluralism and with problems of theological method. The plurality of human believing becomes visible without our resorting to the bifurcations of Western philosophy or dividing experienced wholeness into disjoined parts. In both ways, the federal paradigm points to the covenants of human living.

Covenants and the idea of covenant occupy a central place in the Western tradition because of their importance in the Bible and in the religion of the ancient Hebrews. For Christians, Scripture is divided into the Old and New Covenants. The relation of these covenants provides the connection of Christianity to the Hebrew past from which it emerged, and defines the difference. Covenant permeates the Hebrew Scriptures and the religious consciousness of the Hebrew people. Writes Martin Buber: "*Berith,* covenant, between YWVH and Israel denotes an expansion of the leadership and the following so as to cover every department of the people's life . . . an all-embracing relationship founded as an everlasting bond in the making of the covenant."[3]

Though the notion of covenant in a highly articulated form derives especially from the study of ancient Hebrew religion as it appears in the Old Testament, the covenantal pattern is by no means restricted to that location. It is present in other Semitic societies of the ancient Near East, as George Mendenhall has shown in a work that casts considerable light on the pervasiveness of the covenant form.[4] The covenant appears also among the Germanic tribes that invaded and settled western Europe during the period of the Roman Empire, among North American Indians, and among the Aztecs. Indeed, the covenant seems to be present throughout the tribal structure of primitive societies. It is, for example, difficult to say whether the covenantal or federal theological and political forms that arise in Switzerland are the product more of medieval organization among the Helvetian tribes or of the impact of biblical Christian patterns. Perhaps the widespread character of covenantal social order renders the issue moot. Political federalism as it emerges in Europe and spreads to America is clearly related to both, though the rise of specifically federal political philosophy and social patterns occurs in areas where the federal theology is dominant.[5]

In any event, a covenantal understanding does not necessarily limit us to the biblical tradition but rather is an element in that tradition which relates to what we know of the primitive, tribal character of human society, whether in Europe, Asia, Africa, or the Americas, both ancient and modern. Rather than being restrictive, the covenant provides considerable scope for articulating the patterned wholeness of human experiencing. Here we shall be using it to describe the primal network of commitments in that wholeness which it gives shape and structure.

In the first place, covenant directs attention to the condition of our existence. To the extent that we act in terms of networks of commitments, given their pattern by ultimate commitments governing understanding and decision, we may speak of these commitment patterns as the covenants of personal, social, and historical living. Concerning covenant in the ancient Hebrew context, Johannes Pedersen writes:

> One is born of a covenant and into a covenant, and wherever one moves in life, one makes a covenant or acts on the basis of the already existing covenant. If everything that comes under the term covenant were dissolved, existence would fall to pieces, because no soul can live an isolated life. . . . It can only exist as a link of a whole, and it cannot work and act without working in connection with other souls and through them. Therefore the annihilation of the covenant would not only be the ruin of society, but the dissolution of each individual soul.
>
> The covenant is not a thing to be dealt with as one pleases. It goes deeper than everything else, because it is the presupposition of all life.[6]

Pedersen sees the covenant as fundamental to community and to the existence of each individual in community.

Humans are born into covenants already made and are called to commit themselves to the heritage of their parents' community. Emergence into selfhood is a process of affirming or rejecting the loyalties by which a person will live. In theological terms, becoming a self is a process of choosing the gods we will serve. Do we understand ourselves as Christian because we were so fated by the covenants into which we were born; because we responded to the loving concern of parents, peers, and teachers; or because we choose to see human need, our neighbors, and the call to live in terms of Christian faith? It is both circumstance and choice. We have no loyalties except as we affirm them and stipulate them as rooted in reality. Yet our allegiances cannot be understood apart from the context of concerned interaction surrounding us or apart from the covenants of historical possibilities awaiting the emergence of our awareness.

In the second place, covenant is not only a condition in which we emerge into selfhood and live; covenant also conditions that living. Whether we choose or are chosen, there seems no escape from awareness that the choice of covenants gives shape to our decisions, our future, and the whole of our living.

The structure of human acting is covenantal. In acting, we choose among alternatives present, and these decisions are made in terms of commitments, commitments given pattern and priority by the covenants in which we dwell. Purposes, norms, and relations in a context of commitment inform and condition our decisions and actions.

Language also can be understood in covenantal perspective. In Plato's *Cratylus*, both a conventional and a natural view of language are rejected. Instead it is suggested that language is a social instrument by means of which persons within a linguistic community communicate to one another what they believe is real. That is, language has both the stipulative element of conventional usage and the element of believed-in reality. It is a function of the covenants of human living.

Covenants permit us to expand our awareness of the worlds in which humans live so that, without pretense of rising above the context of experiencing, we may articulate the meaning of these worlds toward their horizons. The covenants of ancient Israel and of primitive tribes refer not only to agreements among persons in community but also to the God or gods in which the tribe believes, to the root metaphor or myth explaining its self-understanding, to the historical duration relating past and future, and to the sovereign reality in which the community believes itself to exist. Covenants shape the particular acts and relations of daily living. But they also proclaim the horizons that provide the total context, the history, and the legitimations within which ordinary activity takes place.

Covenants of human living reach back to *creation*, depicting in myth or saga the origins of the world, the society, and the patterns making up communal reality. Such creation myths do not refer only to some time in the past. They are designed to guide the valuation and the acting of the present. For example, the covenant of creation in the Hebrew-Christian tradition relates the whole of humanity and nature to God with such universal intent as can never be obliterated by the intense particularism of Jewish and Christian sectarianism.

Covenants of human living look forward to *consummation,* to the end of world process and its final shape. Whether circular, linear, or in another form, covenants have an eschatological character that informs the anticipations of every present.

Covenants of human living exhibit a *coherency* of disparate particulars summed up in a *root metaphor,* which enables individuals and communities to engage in the process of continually integrating varied elements into meaningful wholes. We cannot speak of the particulars apart from their integration into wholes or of wholes of experiencing apart from the particulars that are comprehended in them.

Covenants of human living are founded on believed-in *reality,* that final sovereignty or deity that is the source of original creativity, that defines consummation, assures coherence, and to which a root metaphor refers. Humans live, not toward illusion, but toward what they are convinced is actual.

In these ways, covenantal understanding provides a means for understanding one's own community and also other communities of interpretation and faith. In having different patterns of commitment, different histories, other communities are internal to their own covenants, though external to ours. By giving attention to the covenants within which other communities dwell, we may discern their histories, come in some measure to understand them, and perhaps have our own covenants illumined for us.[7] The covenants of human living, thus, pertain to the histories within which humans dwell, to the commitments and loyalties that are the living fabric of

community, to selfhood and gods, and to the fiduciary
foundations of human lives in all their rich variety.

So central and pervasive a place do the covenants of
human living occupy in our experiencing, that they may
well be invisible to us. As with eyeglasses, humans do not
see their covenants but rather see everything through
them. In order to become aware of these covenants, we
must explore our patterns of action and loyalty until we
raise them into consciousness. The pluralistic context of
other communities may aid in making us more aware of
our own covenants.

It is the covenants of human living, whether recognized or not, that give shape to human communities and
action. To understand the wholeness of human experiencing—of individuals or ethnic groups, of nations
or religious communities—it is to the network of
commitments summed up in covenant that we must go.
When we understand the covenants of human living, we
make human worlds in their patterned wholeness and
commitmental power available for theological analysis.

2. Fiduciary Foundations of Knowing

A federal paradigm, understood through the covenants
of human living, changes our perspective on human
knowing. Epistemology is the name philosophers give to
the problem of knowing. We could, therefore, call
knowing, in the federal paradigm, a covenantal epistemology. This perspective discloses the fiduciary foundations
of knowing in two important ways.

First, the federal paradigm changes the traditional
dyadic presuppositions of knowing into a triadic epistemology. In the Western philosophical heritage, knowing
has been regarded almost universally as dyadic, involving
the knower and the known. Descartes, convinced that he
is because he thinks, reduces precise rationality to clear
and distinct ideas and comes up with knowledge. Kant,
assuming a universal, nonhistorical reason, can as

knower show the character and limitations of knowledge. As Whitehead tells us: "The object-subject structure of experience . . . has been identified with the bare relation of knower to known. The subject is the knower, the object is the known. Thus, with this interpretation, the object-subject relation is the known-knower relation."[8] Whitehead does not disagree with the prevailing dyadic epistemology but only with the easy identification of subject-object with knower-known that overlooks the difficulty of achieving knowledge. Within the federal paradigm, the knower is a historical, social being, and knowing is a historical communal enterprise. Whatever is called knowledge is so asserted within a community of interpretation and asserted by persons who are participants within such a community and share its commitments as the basis of any possible warrants of credibility. Knowing is triadic, taking place within the covenants of human living that define communities of interpretation and provide the root metaphors and stories informing human understanding.

Second, a federal paradigm illumines the fiduciary context of knowing. Thinkers in the Western tradition have not only been, with few exceptions, dyadic in epistemology, they have also with near unanimity sought to attain certainty of knowledge that in no way relies upon belief. Belief is generally regarded as an inferior prelude to knowledge for which knowledge, once attained, has no further need. The goal of knowledge for the philosopher, therefore, is a location beyond all fiduciary components, an ontological peak from which to speak final truth in the imperial mood. A covenantal epistemology discloses that all assertions emerge from a complex context of cultural assumptions, intellectual postulates, communally accredited warrants, and commonly accepted data. There is no historian or scientist who is not also a believer, that is, who is not located in some community of interpretation and faith providing the basis for accredited statements and valid conclusions. In federal perspective, it is the task to uncover the network of commitments of varied kinds that form the foundations of whatever is called, in one community or another, knowledge.

In this section, we shall attempt to explain further this covenantal epistemology. In the process, the triadic and fiduciary nature of knowing will become clear.

The wholeness of human experiencing encompasses the activities of walking, seeing, and touching, and also believing, valuing, and knowing. Particulars and comprehensiveness are inseparable from the wholeness in which they appear, a wholeness which is present in our earliest awareness and grows in scope and complexity.

The context in which awareness emerges is relational and social, and in the first instance especially, tactile. The action of touching an infant and of the infant's action of touching in response to tactile stimulation is crucial for its development. This context of relation, action, and interaction mediated especially by touch is also the bearer of meaning, meaning already given pattern and valency by the covenants of human living into which the organism is born and through which social awareness develops into awareness of self related to selves.

Patterned awareness emerges from communal covenants into personal streams of consciousness and then into that greater precision we call knowing. Sense percepts and order, impingement and response, within a field of experiencing already given pattern by our community are present together for us. Our knowing develops into a wholeness of experiencing shaped by covenantal relations, valency, and meaning, in which we are already dwelling as we become aware of their presence. Our responsive involvement in preexisting covenants accompanies our most elementary awareness and knowing.

This emergent wholeness fits better with the triadic notion of interpretation found in Charles Sanders Peirce and Josiah Royce than with the dyadic pattern dominant in Western epistemology. "Interpretation," writes Royce, "always involves a relation of three terms . . . interpretation *is* a triadic relation. . . . One of the three terms is the interpreter; a second term is the object—the person or the meaning or the text—which is interpreted; the third is the person to whom the interpretation is addressed." Interpretation thus is "an explicitly social undertaking" and relies upon a process of interpretation within a community of interpretation that assumes preceding interpretations and anticipates a continuing process of interpretation. Foreshadowing the work of Polanyi and Kuhn, Royce illustrates his point by reference to a scientific community of interpretation within which interpreter and interpretation are held to be real. "Nothing is more concretely known to us than are the nature, the value, and the goals of a community of interpretation," and it is through commitment to and loyalty to such communities that it becomes possible for us to know and to discover.[9]

In the triadic pattern suggested by Royce for a community of interpretation, we distinguish and articulate patterns and particulars in experiencing, not from the encounter of an isolated self with this or that element, but as occasions are interpreted to us from cradle to grave by companions in the communities of interpretations of which we are a part. Whether we refer to a hand and then to my hand, or to a family and then a nation, or to a tree and then to a natural order, we are acting in response to interpretations given us in community. "Through the medium of language, with its names and categories, its grammar and syntax, its logic," writes H. Richard Niebuhr, "I have been introduced to . . . the *system* of nature as *systematized* by society. I classify the events and find their meaning in their relations to each other but do so always with the aid of the *a priori* categories of my social, historical reason, derived from my companions."[10]

R. G. Collingwood speaks of the relative presuppositions upon which any intelligible structure depends and of the absolute presuppositions upon which relative presuppositions depend. Thomas Kuhn, as we have seen, suggests that scientific knowing takes place within a network of commitments or a paradigm. And Michael Polanyi speaks of the fiduciary character of all knowing.

> We must now recognize belief once more as the source of all knowledge. Tacit assent and intellectual passions, the sharing of an idiom and of a cultural heritage, affiliation to a like-minded community: such are the impulses which shape our vision of the nature of things on which we rely for our mastery of things. No intelligence, however critical or original, can operate outside such a fiduciary framework.[11]

There is, then, a covenantal basis for knowing of axioms and postulates, presuppositions and warrants, which are validated by persons and communities committed to them and the knowing dependent upon them.

Knowing, however, is not merely being *given* interpretations by others. Knowing means also active grasping, dwelling in, and reshaping what we receive. The emerging self is first responsively absorbent and then creatively revisionist of the covenants and interpretations given. Knowing is a communal activity that depends upon the network of commitments in which we come to dwell and the transformation of those commitments. Within a covenantal epistemology, therefore, knowing is not merely a given; it is a shared achievement.

Knowing is a skillful activity of persons in which they attend *from* an inclusive covenant held tacitly *to* certain particulars that derive their meaning from the whole and in turn define the whole insofar as it is possible to articulate its meaning. Forgetting the personal involvement in knowing, Western thinkers have pursued "a mistaken ideal of objectivity" and neglected "the fiduciary rootedness of all rationality." Knowing depends on "tacit coefficients" which are sustained and passed on within "a cultural life shared by a community." The acceptance of these tacit components "seals a pact of mutual confidence within the community."[12]

Knowing is also relational. Particulars emerge against a background of related wholeness. A chair *is* a chair by *not being* a table or a tree; a room exists as part of a house; a person becomes known to us within society; every entity appears for us in a relational context. In this perspective there is no fact or entity in our experience that exists apart from its being within a covenantal wholeness which gives meaning to all its parts. This relational characteristic of data in a covenantal epistemology may be contrasted with a positivistic epistemology or what might be called a metaphysic of logical atomism. In these latter views, experience comes in small, objective packages regarded as having greater reality than any more encompassing experience. Whether it is the stone that is most real or the hardness and color is open to debate. But for the metaphysic of logical atomism either stone or its hardness is more real than the performance of a Beethoven sonata by a pianist or the commitment to a cause. As Michael Polanyi reminds us, "Unbridled lucidity can destroy our understanding of complex matters. . . . The belief that, since particulars are more tangible, their knowledge offers a true conception of things is fundamentally mistaken."[13] In a covenantal epistemology, there is no experience of a stone or its hardness without a more encompassing framework of meaning within which these particulars are interpreted. And there is no belief in the reality of the particulars apart from the commitment to that encompassing wholeness as real. Emphasizing the evaluative significance of experience but not differing on the central issue, Kenneth Boulding writes, "For any individual organism or organization, there are no such things as 'facts.' There are only messages filtered through a changeable value system."[14]

3. Dwelling In and Breaking Out

To exist in the covenants of human living involves not only patterns of commitment and knowing but also total immersion within the whole, dwelling in the covenantal world. We dwell in the covenant as we live in our bodies or utilize our mother tongue. By the act of indwelling, the covenant becomes a constitutive element of ourselves. It permeates our living, at once affirming the personal quality of our acts and the communal dimension of our experiencing.

Viewed in this way, covenantal indwelling provides a basis for understanding the cohesiveness of human society. Humans in a community share a cultural heritage as well as a biological one. And the shared culture evokes powerful common commitments, so that personal existence must be regarded as a communally interwoven fabric in which individuals share a covenantal solidarity.

But covenantal indwelling also suggests a way to understand changing cultural and social perspectives. To dwell in a covenant with full intensity involves the possibility of breaking out toward new, more comprehensive meanings. Covenants are not static but evolving and developing; as communities break out toward an unfolding future, their histories and their worlds change.

The contrast between a static and a covenantal view is illustrated in the mystery stories of A. Conan Doyle and those of Agatha Christie. In the stories by Doyle, there is a static world of facts. To solve a mystery, Sherlock Holmes collects a sufficient amount of data to construct the truth about a situation that was puzzling. This is an understanding of history and the world informed by the traditional Western paradigm. In the Christie stories about Hercule Poirot, reality has a more elusive, shifting quality. Data surrounding the mystery or the murder are there, but they take on different meaning and valency in relation to different total perspectives into which they may be absorbed. Whereas for Holmes there is a single true pattern to be discovered by placing fact on fact, for Poirot there are quite different ways in which it is possible to integrate the clues related to the mystery. Agatha Christie leads her readers on by inviting them to dwell in first one and then another integration of particulars into a whole. The resolution at the end of the story provides a surprise as Poirot breaks out to an unexpected integration of data that is more inclusive and more artistically satisfying (see especially the fascinating "solution" in *Murder on the Orient Express*).

Our understanding of the past exhibits this shifting character of dwelling in and breaking out, as our perspective changes or our evaluation of certain sources alters. The notion that the past is a static matter to which the future must conform or which produces the future in a deterministic manner cannot survive acquaintance with the changing past to which various histories and historians open us. New documents or data do not merely provide additional "facts." Instead they may alter the entire perspective of the historian, modify every particular in the field of viewing, and change the historian's appraisal of the meaning of the past. In similar fashion, not only new data related to the past, but also new occurrences in the present may alter the field of valency for historians or for a national community, thus changing the meaning of all particulars. `The Japanese attack on Pearl Harbor did nothing in one sense to alter the relationships between Britain and the United States. In another sense, however, it altered every part of that relationship by changing the field of valency in America; after Pearl Harbor, the British were no longer a people in trouble but rather vital allies in a struggle for survival. "Experience," William James reminds us, "has ways of *boiling over* and making us correct our present formulas."[15]

Discussions about the quest for the "historical Jesus" and many arguments over the resurrection suffer, not because there is disagreement over documents, data, and procedure, but because there is a difference of perspective between those holding a *bruta facta* understanding of human experiencing and those who understand human experiencing as a fabric of meaning and interpretation within communities of interpretation. The former seek to "break through" the New Testament documents to the "objective facts." The latter know only alternative totalities of meaning that give different significance to particulars integrated into each perspective.[16]

If we are to understand more fully what it means to dwell in and break out, however, we must seek to articulate covenantal epistemology with reference to the ascending and descending levels of comprehensiveness of the entities included within it.

In the wholeness of our experiencing, we are aware not only of diverse elements included in a total pattern but also of patterns of greater and lesser inclusiveness, of some patterns that exclude others, and some that partly include and partly exclude others. A university includes libraries, classrooms, and laboratories. Selves include bodies, minds, and communally shared histories. These are examples of ascending and descending levels of comprehensiveness (see Polanyi, *The Tacit Dimension,* pp. 33-44).

Entities of which we are aware comprehend other entities and may in turn be particulars within more comprehensive entities. When we say "table," we are engaging in an action of knowing by means of which we have integrated certain particulars into a whole. We have integrated experiences of wood and tactile contact, color and shape, origin and function, and the like into the entity we then refer to as a table. But each of these entities comprehended in "table" itself includes certain particulars and so also is a comprehensive entity. What we call wood comprehends certain texture, origin, use, relation. So also with what we call color, shape, and so on. In ascending order, a table may be comprehended in the entity called "room," which in turn may be comprehended in "city," and so on. Or "table" is also comprehended in the entity we call furniture, which in turn is comprehended in what we call physical entities, and so on. It is for this reason that Gilbert Ryle's "category mistake," or confusion about levels of comprehensiveness, is at the bottom of much disagreement over interpretation.

When we focus on any particular, we bring our entire wholeness of experience to bear on that entity. And it is only by virtue of that wholeness of culture, thought, and language implicit in the activity of knowing, that we are enabled to integrate the relevant elements and identify the object before us. Oneness, individuality, that which makes up an entity in our experiencing, involves the action of integrating many particulars within a more encompassing whole. Knowing is a covenantal activity, with entities appearing as we bind component parts into a whole. Knowing is a covenantal activity in that each action of knowing is dependent upon the communal covenants of interpretation that inform the comprehensive wholeness of our experiencing.

A problem arises, however, when by social habit or philosophic convention, we attribute ontological priority to a certain level of comprehensiveness. In positivistic movements, for example, ontological priority is accorded to what can be called the common-sense or everyday level of experiencing; tables and chairs and rocks acquire superior reality to embarrassment and anxiety, to selves and gods. But it would appear that the common-sense level exists in virtue of its relation to and location within a patterned wholeness of experiencing.

A further problem occurs when a reality is alleged to be *beyond* and *separate from* the wholeness of human experiencing and is asserted to have ontological priority over experienced entities. These allegations may refer to an otherworldly spiritual realm or to a wholly-other deity, to Being itself or to a substantial reality underlying appearances. While there would appear to be no perspective from which to declare such assertions false, there would also seem to be no basis for declaring them to be true. Epistemology, seen as a human meaning for knowing, cannot satisfy our craving for final knowledge outside a tacit, fiduciary context, that is, apart from the covenants of human living. How are we to attain a location outside these human covenants, which give birth to all our knowing, in order to provide the final validations required in correspondence theories of knowledge or allegations about realms beyond what is experienced?

A FEDERAL PARADIGM

Despite its limitations, epistemology can aid in understanding the patterns of comprehensive entities that comprise our experience and assist in uncovering the activity of tacit integration that makes up our knowing. In so doing, it discloses the commitments that shape these acts of integration and the covenantal wholeness that informs our knowing and provides the horizons of our living.

But the covenantal paradigm not only comprehends the past, it also points toward the future. We discover that we dwell in our inherited faith in order to break out toward an emerging future. At this point a covenantal epistemology points beyond cohesion and stasis toward change, toward intellectual discovery, and toward liberation. Liberation emerges in this perspective, not only as a goal to be sought and a process in which humanity develops, but also as a methodological principle for discerning and defining theological transformation.

In the perspective provided by the covenantal paradigm, religious commitment and faith in God means dwelling in and breaking out. We belong to one horizon of believing even as we are being liberated toward another. H. Richard Niebuhr calls this breaking out "the conversion and permanent revolution of our human religion."[17] Infused with hope, we are discovering the human journey from the homeland of the inherited past toward the homeland of the oncoming future. Covenant faith emphasizes communal memory and loyalty within which we grow to selfhood, and at the same time draws us toward a future of anticipated liberation. Covenant *means* liberation, and liberation provides the criterion to measure movement and to discern a pattern of faithfulness when the gods change.

X.

THE GODS
OF HUMAN
BELIEVING

"I decided to subordinate great theological thoughts, like
those of Thomas Aquinas and Karl Barth, to the
intellectual and spiritual needs of the farmers," writes
Kosuke Koyama. "I am forced to make this decision
because of my involvement with the farmers." Thus does
Koyama announce his participation in theological transformation. But the change makes Koyama sound more
biblical than the great theological thoughts he pushes
aside. "Is not involvement the only soil from which
theology germinates? . . . The theology for northern
Thailand begins and grows in northern Thailand, and
nowhere else," he continues. "Northern Thailand theology, the theology that serves Jesus Christ in northern
Thailand, will surely come into being when we dare to
make this decision."[1] Theology emerges not from distant
systems, but from within the covenants of human living.
It is there that the gods of human believing take shape in
the needs and aspirations of persons in community.

For the federal paradigm, the covenant provides the
means for understanding human action within the
context of community, history, nature, and God. A
covenantal epistemology offers a way to understand
human knowing within the wholeness of experiencing.
And the theological principle of liberation illumines the

pattern of history as humans dwell in their past in order to break out toward a future of unthinkable consummation. The covenant of Christian faith is given shape and content through the stories, proclamations, and parables brought to focus in the life, teachings, death, and resurrection of Jesus Christ. Jesus Christ is the root metaphor of the federal paradigm, understood in Christian perspective. But this paradigm also permits us to understand faith perspectives of other communities and thus to deal with the pluralistic context of human believing.

If pluralism is to become manageable and the federal paradigm is to be adequately articulated, two concepts are crucial—religion and deity. What meaning can be given these terms that will encompass the variety of human believing yet remain within communal historical perspective? How can religion and deity be reconceptualized without assuming a universal point of view or reducing the variety of faiths to fit a single definition?

To begin, we must limit ourselves to human meaning. The federal paradigm relates to human locations of acting and believing. Our convictions about what is real and valuable emerge in a communal context of believing and are grounded in that believing. We have noted that philosophers and theologians alike sometimes forget their human locations and assume that they can rise above all historical context to an absolute standpoint. Christian faith does not turn a believer, even the theologian, into God. The proclamation that Jesus Christ is the Way, the Truth, and the Life seems to me a confession of Christian faith that adjudges Christians as well as others as *not being* the Way, the Truth, and the Life. In the same way, philosophers cannot escape the fiduciary foundations of their knowing; nor does any way appear for other humans to attain to absolute location.

In speaking of a human meaning, however, I do not mean to evade responsibility for making judgments about what appears in my experience, in the experience of the community of interpretation of which I am a part, or in the experience of other persons and other communities as these are reported. Human finitude requires making judgments and committing ourselves through actions. There seems no way to avoid an intention toward finality in every decision, whether trivial or momentous. But we can take special care to remain constantly aware of the soil in which our commitments germinated, of the limitations of our perspectives and our capabilities. Human meaning, as I intend the phrase, refers to the constant responsibility to remember and to make clear the communal convictions, conceptual presuppositions, and personal commitment that underlie our assertions as humans. Human meaning involves judgments about what we believe to be true and not true, what appears to us to be more and less adequate to the wholeness of our experience. But human meaning also involves carefully resisting the temptation to pretend that our judgments are based upon a suprahistorical perspective rather than made from a fiduciary context within a particular community. It is from such a location that I speak of human believing and human meaning.

1. A Human Meaning for Religion

Thomas Luckmann levels a sharp critique at the sociology of religion that "uncritically takes it for granted that church and religion are identical."[2] And I have said that conventional theology suffers from a similar ecclesiastical limitation. How is religion to be understood as part of a transformed theology, as a component of the federal paradigm?

Rather than be applicable only to some particular form of religion, a reconceptualized notion must be adequate for the incredible array of religiousness suggested in any discussion of the reappearance of the gods. But it must be capable of more, as William A. Christian points out. In addition, it "should yield some criteria for recognizing novel forms of religion," that is, forms that would otherwise be invisible. "Suppose the domain of religion were defined simply by pointing to [the major] systems. Then we would have no way of recognizing novel forms of religion, although, from the history of religion, we have good reason to expect some to emerge."[3]

In spite of the importance and magnitude of the problem, it is still amazing how much writing is done on old religions and new religions with inadequate attention, or none, to what is meant when the term religion is used. Some writers seem unaware that any problem exists; after all, they mean what everyone in *their* cultural enclave calls religion.[4] Others evade the issue by uncritically stipulating their own meanings; this approach usually has the virtue at least of clarity, regardless of how inadequate the meaning may be.

Another way to conceptualize religion involves the critical search for "the correct definition." This is to misunderstand the problem. Defining religion is much like attacking a magnetic field with a cookie cutter. Those who demand a definition would do well to heed the warning of William James when he said that the fact that definitions of religion "are so many and so different from one another is enough to prove that the word 'religion' cannot stand for any single principle or essence, but is rather a collective name."[5]

Rather than by definition, religion must be approached through a comprehensive conceptualization based upon diversity of cultural locations. Wilfred Cantwell Smith provides one of the most helpful studies on the way toward such a comprehensive understanding. He warns against reifying "religion" because this implies a static entity (or static entities) which violates the dynamic character of religious believing. He thinks that religiousness should be understood through evolving *traditions* and changing *faith*; in this way we can approach human believing in its variety and fullness.[6]

In the federal paradigm, religion permeates the covenants of human living—individually, socially, culturally. The process of commitment by which tactile, visual, and aural experiences are integrated into the comprehensive entity we call a table has its counterpart in the social process of commitment by means of which the particulars of experience are continuously integrated into the wholeness of communal action, selfhood, society, world, history, and reality making up a religion. One can no more answer "none" when questioned about one's religion than one could answer "none" when asked one's age. To inhabit human location is to have religious commitments as surely as to be human involves being so many years old.

As it binds the differentiated elements and levels of human action and actuality into wholes, religious commitment pervades human experiencing. But it is not identical with experience. What we are designating here as religious concerns the field of force *ordering* human action. This ordering takes place as commitments govern actions and disclose the faith of the agents. Commitments of higher valency set the pattern of lesser commitments and thus reveal the believing and valuing of an action system. Religious faith is no more separable from human living than is design from a building. An architect may make marks on paper to guide the builders, but the design is the pattern of steel and stones, the pattern of functions and relations that shapes the construction, and *is* the finished building. We may examine a constellation of iron filings from many perspectives—their chemical composition, their number, the geometrical shapes they exhibit, or the artistic pattern of their arrangement. Or we may seek to understand the magnetic field of force that controls the pattern of their appearing. In similar fashion, one may study human action from varied perspectives—political, chemical, artistic, or psychological. Religion is to human action much as magnetic fields are to groups of iron filings. To study fields of human action in theological perspective is to examine the pattern of commitments that inform its components in order to discover the religious commitments, those ultimate commitments that shape the whole and point to its god or gods.[7]

THE GODS OF HUMAN BELIEVING

Human actions reflect many commitments, but not all commitments are religious. Our first task must be to distinguish *religious* commitment from other commitments.

Commitments are of varying kinds and degrees. Some are very limited in the obligation incurred. One may be committed to a luncheon engagement or to go with a friend to a movie. Some commitments are longer range and less casual—a financial agreement to contribute to a church or a hospital, or a promise to take a particular stand over a period of time. On an even more comprehensive level of commitment there are marriage covenants, basic vocational directions, loyalty to societal entities such as nations, decisions about the purposes of one's life. In this range of commitment, fundamental loyalties and personal identity are at stake.

Commitments in these varying ranges are made by persons in their societal involvements and also by communities. The commitments among people, states, and federal governments are in part embodied in constitutions, in part in legal codes, and in part in a body of interpersonal agreements and historical understandings, which could never be given full articulation. A treaty between nations involves solemn commitments upon which the anticipation of future actions is based.

We recognize ascending levels of commitment and acknowledge that persons and communities must act in terms of the more important commitments. When we are committed to a luncheon engagement, we are expected to keep it under ordinary circumstances. But no one would question our integrity if we failed to keep a casual luncheon appointment because our spouse was suddenly taken ill or an important conference involving the future of our livelihood intervened.

The patterns of individual and group action manifest an ordering of commitments. In every situation of decision, the particulars are integrated into a pattern of priorities on the basis of a tacit field of commitments. This ordering and integration of particulars takes place within a context of believing, trusting, and valuing that we tacitly assume. This network of commitments may be appropriately called a covenant if one understands it as a field of agency governed by loyalties and commitments.

Every level of commitment in such an interrelated network has religious implications, but only the most comprehensive level is to be designated as religious. Religious commitment extends beyond other levels of commitment in importance and controlling function. It comprehends subordinate commitments and refers to the most encompassing levels of trusting, valuing, valency, identity, and reality present to persons and communities. Religious commitment denotes that level of commitment which takes priority over other levels, and orders all these lesser commitments making up the fabric of human action. Religious commitment refers to the *ultimate* commitment of persons and communities.

By calling this commitment *ultimate,* we must take care to be precise in our meaning. The notion of ultimate commitment can be used normatively, with some particular ultimate in mind. Thus, Ernst Troeltsch at one time regarded Christianity as the ultimate religion, the "culmination-point" toward which all religion moves. Or again, Radhakrishnan takes Indian mysticism as the true ultimate and therefore places Christianity on a lower level. Paul Tillich appears to have a similarly normative notion of the ultimate in speaking of ultimate concern; only when concern has reached what Tillich regards as ultimate is it really ultimate.[8] Later he writes what may suggest a change on this issue: "Religion is the state of being grasped by an ultimate concern, a concern which qualifies all other concerns as preliminary and which itself contains the answer to the question of the meaning of our life."[9]

When I speak of ultimate commitment, I mean whatever is the final encompassing commitment of particular persons or communities. From another perspective, that commitment may appear superficial rather than ultimate. Anyone who takes seriously the ultimate commitments enjoined by the great religious traditions will regard ultimate commitment to pleasure or money or nation as somewhat restricted. Nevertheless, if these commitments are the genuinely final ones for some person or community, then they are *ultimate* for them.

There is close relationship among different levels of commitment. They form a pattern, a dwelt-in covenant in terms of which we act. It is this covenant, this network of commitments, as ordered by ultimate commitments functioning to shape a human field of action, that is primary when we speak of religion. The commitmental configuration of personal, social, and cultural action systems is what we examine in the study of religion. Religion cannot be reified or objectified, but it can be studied.

A federal paradigm provides the means for a reasonably precise conceptualization of religion. By focusing on human commitments and actions, whatever form these take, this conceptualization avoids the more obvious problems of ethnocentric definition. Yet it can be related closely to the Judeo-Christian tradition and thus be accessible to Western theology and the study of religion. By beginning with whatever patterns exist for particular individuals and social groups, this view can take account of the plural character of human believing and open to investigation a much wider spectrum of religious faiths than do the ecclesiastical, conventional notions that have dominated much religious thought in Europe and America.

The focus on the pattern of commitments and action as the clues to ultimate convictions permits us to deal with the relation of religion and change, both retrospectively as it has occurred and prospectively as change takes place. Alteration in older traditions and the emergence of new forms of religion can be discerned. The notions of changing gods and theological transformation are possibilities within a federal paradigm because religion is viewed through historical and social manifestations of human believing rather than in terms of static pre-suppositions. The material for theology and the study of religion derives from what people are actually doing and believing rather than from an orthodoxy that asserts in advance what they ought to believe. This paradigm affirms the human location both of those who study religion, in their own believing, and also those whose faith is being studied.

Most interesting of all, the federal paradigm with its recognition of the diversity and changing character of human believing opens the way to understanding the phenomenon of liberation in theological and ethical perspective. As the permanent revolution of human believing becomes clearer, the centrality of dwelling in and breaking out for religious faith emerges into view. Liberation is not foreign to human religion unless it is restricted to static definitions. In covenantal perspective, liberation becomes a central theme in theology rather than one excluded by restrictive definitions.

2. A Human Meaning for God

In parallel fashion, human meaning for God must take account of the multiple deities present in human believing as well as the decisive quality of God for those who adhere to a deity. This ambiguity is not incidental but crucial for theology. To comprehend diversity without relinquishing the decisive significance of a particular deity for believers, let us begin by saying that gods are present to human believing as the focus of ultimate commitment and loyalty governing action for persons in community. We must remember that a god becomes God in human believing. Perspective and location are functions of believed-in deity; and gods are present decisively for some perspectives and locations, not for others. From the view of one community of faith, the god of the other community is an idol. With this understanding, I can suggest a human meaning for God in covenantal perspective.

First, what can be called the God or the gods of a particular sphere of human experiencing and action functions as *center of trust and value*. Therefore, God is that which shapes trusting and valuing in that realm of actuality. In arguing against calling Christianity "faith" and all other great belief systems "religions," Wilfred Cantwell Smith points out that faith is also at the heart of Islam and all of the world religions. And H. Richard Niebuhr writes: "To have faith and to have a god is one and the same thing."[10]

When we speak of faith in God, we do not mean faith as assent *(assensus)* to a proposition or as the conviction that something exists, but rather an active relying upon *(fiducia)*. God means that in which human beings trust. We may believe that a bank exists but not entrust our money to it. Or we may agree that a footbridge across a mountain chasm is actually there but not trust it sufficiently to venture onto it. The word "god," then, can best be understood as referring primarily to the locus of ultimate reliance from which persons and communities derive their understanding of what is to be trusted in their world and among themselves and their companions.

God is not only a focus of trusting but also of valuing, whether this be self or nation or sex or one of the more complex gods of the world religions. God means what humans rely upon for the significance and worth of their existence. God means that which is valued most and also that which shapes the value-structure by which humans place relative value on all other events, persons, and things. Niebuhr writes: "We never merely believe that life is worth living, but always think of it as made worth living by something on which we rely. And this being, whatever it is, is properly our god."[11]

In functioning as center of trust and value, a god has impact on those who believe. To rely and to value are terms relating to human living. What one relies upon and values ultimately shapes the entire pattern of one's action. As centers of trust and value, therefore, the gods indicate that which has valency, influence, or power in shaping human action.

Second, what humans trust and value invests believers' lives with *meaning*. Faith in God gives a world in which believers dwell, a world with relations and patterns of valency, a world as an arena of action, and a world of a remembered past and anticipated future. Such meaning goes beyond making rational sense of the world, though it is not necessarily dissociated from reasoning. The mother's caress of love has incalculable meaning for the infant. A kiss may give meaning to forgiveness beyond the power of explanations.

It is not without significance that the most enduring theologies have been stories that provide action patterns rather than the more philosophical theologies, which we often think are the only authentic forms theology can take. The various scriptures that convey meaning for the great religions of the world are characterized more by story and dramatic recital than by systematic theology. Indeed, because of this characteristic, scriptures and the religions of which they form a part resist systematic treatment. The addresses and writings most likely to stir political communities also resemble recital of the remembered deeds of the past and their promise for the future. Story, drama, art—engaging the whole of experiencing in faith—evoke loyalty and action.

In this perspective meaning relates to deity as that tacit dimension within which we dwell and to which we are committed. It is by virtue of that encompassing commitment to meaning that we are able to make the smaller commitments of tacit integration required both in communicating meaning and in receiving it.

Third, those who believe do not regard themselves as having faith in faith. That to which they attach themselves in ultimate commitment is trusted in as transcending them and their companions and as being the most *sovereign reality* in the wholeness of experiencing. Human living is toward a believed-in reality, not toward what is regarded as illusion. Those of one community of interpretation may from that perspective affirm the folly of the other's faith; but the believers believe it to be real. Theologians may construct hypothetical gods for their own purposes, but there are no hypothetical gods in human believing. To have a god is to be convinced of and rely upon the reality of that deity.

God as transcending reality especially affirms the future dimension of deity. The real includes not only past and present but also the not-yet. This anticipation of consummation in the future is so deeply imbedded in Judeo-Christian thought that one wonders how it can have been obscured by dogmatic formulations limiting divine purpose and sovereignty to the past. It seems strange that Marxist influence has been required to remind Christians of what seems so central to their heritage. The explanation apparently is that eschatological hope became the property of fringe movements. Institutionalized religion of the dominant majority emphasized the finished, static character of divine action, concealing the possibility of uncontrolled, revolutionary power in God behind such mystifying phrases as The Divine Decree. Whatever the faith, those who believe are directing attention to a reality transcending the present; they are living toward the hidden possibilities of the future; they are proclaiming concepts and power that remain to be unfolded in an emerging not-yet.

God as transcending reality also points to liberation. Clearly, in the major faiths of the world, the sovereign reality upon which believers rely is a source of deliverance. The hope for liberation does not rest exclusively with the abilities of oppressed groups to win freedom. This hope is rooted in the conviction that the thrust of divine power is toward justice and toward deliverance from all that enslaves humanity. "My God is a God who frees people," proclaimed Antoinette Brown, the first woman ordained by a Congregational church in the United States.[12] Such faith in God derives from the past and points toward the future. The sovereign power

making for liberation is not transcendent in the sense of
being "above" and unrelated to history, but transcendent
in utilizing the force of nations, political movements, and
familial community to break the bonds of oppression.

In these ways—as center of trust, value, and power, as
focus of meaning, and as transcending reality—a human
meaning for God emerges into view.

3. God: Projection, Discovery, and Revelation

In order to clarify further the meaning of the federal
paradigm, let us pose a question. Is God to be understood
as human projection, as discovery, or as revealed? And
then let us question the question. Is it necessary to regard
these three alternatives as mutually exclusive? Must we
choose one and reject the other two?

Not at all. In our quest for a human meaning for God as
part of a federal paradigm, it appears not only impossible
to choose among these alternatives but also necessary to
affirm all three. Projection, discovery, and revelation are all
crucial to the illumination of the significant dimensions of
human believing in deity.

God as Projection. The view that faith in deity is a
projection of human believing and aspiration has taken
various forms. Marxism depicts faith in God as a
projection of social power designed by the strong to keep
the masses subjugated to the authority of dominant
ecclesiastical and political groups. Sigmund Freud sees
deity as the projection of human psychic needs and
conflicts. Emil Durkheim represents still another type of
projectionism in seeing deity as the extension and vivid
personification of the structures and norms of a given
society.

One of the most important figures holding the
projectionist viewpoint is Ludwig Feuerbach (1804–
1872). Central to Feuerbach's thought is the notion that
belief in God or gods is a projection of basic human
aspirations. Feuerbach appreciates the encompassing

significance of gods for human life. But for him, the referent of language about God is to be found in the deepest impulses of the human spirit, not in any reality prior to or apart from humanity itself. Gods are the hopes of humans projected onto the limits of their world.

Belief in gods, in Feuerbach's view, is not peripheral to human life but emerges from its very center and permeates its entire surge toward fulfillment. He recognizes that religious faith arises from the core of existence and expresses the wholeness of our humanity. God defines the limits of humanity's upward thrust beyond nature and extends the sphere of existence more widely than a naturalistic view of humanity allows. It is by means of faith in a god that humans live in an expanded transnatural world. "Faith in the beyond," Feuerbach contends, "derives from faith in the freedom of subjectivity from the limits of nature—consequently, it is faith of humans in themselves."[13]

But the outer limits of this wider world to which faith in gods opens humanity cannot be specified with precision. The gods projected in faith define particular spaces of existence but not the final limits of human aspiration and possibility. Gods open up cultural space for humans and permit them to be human, with human spheres of meaning and purpose. Gods beyond these gods may represent projective power which will burst through the bounds of spheres previously occupied by humanity. Even as religion is a vehicle for human transcendence over nature, so also it is a vehicle for continuing self-transcendence, suggesting the hidden depth of humanity and the unknown future beyond present projections which may open themselves. Thus, for Feuerbach, "the mystery of religion is the mystery of the essence of humanity itself. "

Not only did Feuerbach perceive the relation of faith in gods to the deepest and most pervasive characteristics of humanity, he also related the divine to the widest horizons and emergent potentialities of the human future. His perspective and analysis illumine our experiencing and expand our understanding of religious faith, even though his view of what he has described with great insight as projection seems to cross the bounds of what it is possible for a human to affirm with finality. Such conclusions could be reached only if Feuerbach occupied a location outside his own humanity and history.

God as Discovery. Important as the projectionist view of faith may be in demonstrating believed-in gods as the most comprehensive horizons of human commitment and identity, this perspective alone fails to do justice to the complexity and depth of religion. In human believing there is also a heuristic surge of faith that constantly tests the boundaries defined by cumulative experiencing, presses against these dwelt-in horizons with a curious mixture of faith and doubt, and repeatedly breaks through these limits toward an unknown future. God, for religious faith, means discovery as well as projection.

On the one hand, religion binds experiencing into a stable whole that lends coherence to individual, social, and cultural action. On the other hand, religious faith has a revolutionary impulse within it producing rebellion and reformulation within religious movements, seemingly in direct proportion to their vitality. Entwined inseparably with political and economic elements of society and encompassing them, human believing proves itself again and again to be a powerful source both of the stability that resists change and also of the dynamism producing revolution. Gods viewed in human perspective are never static and unchanging, for the same ultimate commitment that lends the appearance of finality to faith also impels the believers beyond the horizons defined by their dogmas.

Michael Polanyi speaks of this impulse of faith toward change. Heuristic passion, says Polanyi, empowers and guides the creative endeavors of humanity and impels humans to venture ceaselessly toward the new, toward the unknown. Thus human community lives ever on the verge of discovery, poised between the driving promise of past fulfillment and the magnetic anticipation of further fulfillment drawing us toward the promise of the future.

For Polanyi, human living in its fullest dimensions means dwelling in and breaking out. Humans dwell in a world when they believe in its reality and live with commitment toward that reality. But living with creativity means dwelling in one's world with a passion which seeks beyond it. Thus dwelling-in verges constantly on breaking out of one's world and coming to dwell in a world of wider horizons. Every human horizon proves temporary. Human life, however settled it appears to be in its everyday routines, is ultimately a nomadic existence. The lure of the unknown, the promise of the future, are both the sources and the manifestions of human creativity. Humanity moves through projection toward discovery.

God as Revelation. The concepts of projection and discovery do not do full justice to the sense of reality in religious faith, nor do they explain the sense that this reality breaks in upon us no less than we break out toward it. God appears in human believing as center of trust and value and as ever-expanding meaning, but even more as transcending reality that grasps us in our movements of discovery and reshapes our world with irresistible, revolutionary power. God means the projection of total selfhood, the heuristic passion toward discovery, *and* also the in-breaking of revelation.

Nowhere is this understanding of God described with greater insight and sensitivity than by H. Richard Niebuhr. No work on theology in our time can be complete that does not deal with Niebuhr and the issues he raises. In particular, any treatment of revelation that does not draw deeply on Niebuhr's insights will seem pale, even superficial. In *The Meaning of Revelation,* increasingly recognized as a turning point in twentieth-century theology, Niebuhr rejects the older notions of static relevation, the residue of which is carefully controlled by the ecclesiastical establishment; he is also critical of the nineteenth-century liberal notion of revelation that resolves God into the highest peak of human believing. God cannot be understood exclusively through the dogmatic formulations of the past or through a phenomenology of faith. Belief in God is an ever-present faith, giving unity to the events of personal and communal living.

We come to this perspective, Niebuhr suggests, not by rising above our history and divesting ourselves of our humanity, but rather through particular experiences in our communal and personal lives that impress us so strongly as to call forth commitment, give a conviction of reality, and provide a sense of coherent meaning. This is revelation. "Revelation," writes Niebuhr, "means for us that part of our inner history which illumines the rest of it." Or again, "Revelation means . . . an event in our history which brings rationality and wholeness into the confused joys and sorrows of personal existence and allows us to discern order in the brawl of communal histories. . . . Through this happening we are enabled to apprehend what we are, what we are suffering and doing and what our potentialities are."[14]

Such events and happenings, however, are not final and definitive. Revelatory events occur again and again, disclosing the newness of the future, reshaping the meanings of the past, and requiring the radical reconstruction of human believing. "Revelation is . . . the revolution in our thought about divine power," writes Niebuhr. Revelation means "permanent revolution of our human religion,"[15] which draws us toward change and liberation with the power of total faith, and impels us at the same time to push against the limits of our conceptual schemes, thus drawing us beyond the patterns of commitment in which we dwell toward new horizons of believing and acting. Revelation means permanent revolution in our awareness of the divine reality in which we live and move and have our being. Revelation emphasizes the human quality of religious faith and the continuing process of changing gods. In the perspective of Christian faith, the permanent revolution of revelatory consciousness means an ever-renewing, continuously liberating faith, not in different gods, but in the God who is becoming, who is Lord of all histories, sovereign of the changing past and also of all possible futures, the foundation of human hope who can never be contained within the formulations of the past.

In covenantal perspective, God must be understood by means of projection, discovery, and revelation. With this view, we are able now to explore the relation of pluralism and liberation in a transformed theology, that is, a theology that germinates, as Koyama reminds us, in the soil of human location, in the covenants of human living.

XI.

PLURALISM
AND LIBERATION

"In our time, contributions to Christian Theology of Liberation have been forthcoming out of the most diverse quarters of misery in our fragmented world," write Jürgen Moltmann and Elisabeth Moltmann-Wendel. "It is possible that *liberation theology* will become a new ecumenical point of convergence for the most different traditions, experiences and struggles."[1] In a world of plural traditions and multiple oppressions, Christian theology could take no more important or more fruitful direction. This seems to be true for several reasons.

First, liberation theology takes up with renewed vigor the theme of deliverance from bondage that resounds through the Bible. The Exodus, as Yahweh's liberating action on behalf of the Hebrews, forms the core of the covenant, of faith, and of history for Israel. The prophets continue the theme of liberation, using it as the basis for judging Israel and the ground of the hope for the covenant people. Jesus opens his ministry with the proclamation from Isaiah of deliverance to the captives (Luke 4). Paul interprets the Christian message as liberation from bondage to the law of sin and death (Rom. 8:2); indeed the whole "creation itself will be set free from its bondage to decay and obtain the glorious liberty of the children of God" (Rom. 8:21). In the Bible, salvation means liberation in all its dimensions.

Second, liberation theology places Christians on the side of the poor and the oppressed. The Judeo-Christian movement has been the source of many new surges of liberation from ancient times to the present. Since its societal triumph under Constantine, however, the Christian church has more often been on the side of the oppressor than of the oppressed. One example can be seen in the increasing subjugation of women by the church following its release from persecution by the Roman Empire.[2] The emergence of liberation theology aids in the continuing struggle to liberate the Christian movement from idolatrous relations with the principalities and powers of this world. The rich and the powerful are not to be rejected. But relation to all oppressors and oppressive societal structures must be utilized for social change and to obtain liberation for the oppressed rather than in order to approve or preserve oppressive political, economic, and ecclesiastical conditions. Liberation theology, therefore, aids Christianity in recovering and maintaining its biblical message.

Third, liberation theology has provided ways to relate Christianity and Marxism in the struggle for liberation. The close ties of the Christian churches to the capitalist and post-capitalist economies in Europe and America have been challenged. Limited alliances between Christians and Marxists on behalf of human liberation have become possible. Political space has been opened up to permit an easing of tensions between the communist East and the democratic West. Many Christians have learned from Marxist sources the old biblical conviction of the inseparability of faith and action, of theory and praxis, in the cause of liberation.

Though fruitful in many ways, liberation theology has not been without its difficulties. One phase of liberation theology, the so-called theology of revolution, for example, was politically naïve. It pitted eschatological dreams against military force and sometimes assisted regimes into power that were more oppressive than their predecessors. Some forms of liberation theology have tended, like the lady who rode on the tiger, to be swallowed by Marxism, and thus left unable to distinguish the helpful from the harmful elements for liberation in that varied and ambiguous movement. And at times, liberation has seemed to become more a slogan than a goal.

Perhaps the most serious problem of liberation theology, however, has been the tendency to view one form of the theology of liberation (e.g. Latin American) as the only one, to ignore the varied theologies of liberation around the world, and to forget the history of liberation in Asia, in Africa, in the Americas, and in Europe. The theology of liberation does not exist in one location, nor is it the invention of this generation. Its meaning and its power become clear when seen not in a single manifestation, but in its historical and global pluralism.

Whatever its difficulties, the liberation movement today has aided in breaking the spell of the Constantinian past in Christian theology, in sharpening world awareness of rising demands for social justice, and in rediscovering the old insight that biblical faith includes eschatological anticipations of newness, change, and liberation. To carry these insights forward as liberation becomes a central principle of transformed theology, it is helpful to explore the symbiotic relationship of pluralism and liberation.

1. The Liberating Power of Pluralism

Theologians caught in the Constantinian paradigm have usually viewed pluralism as a manifestation of secularism. Van Harvey, for example, writes: "Pluralism is, I believe, but just another aspect of secularism and the problem it poses for theology."[3] Such a perspective misses the vital interdependence of pluralism and liberation.

PLURALISM AND LIBERATION

There are those, too, who reject the pluralistic dimensions of liberation. "That in a pluralistic society there are countless ways of being pluralistic in the church and thus also as regards the starting point of theology, should be clear," writes Frederick Herzog. "Liberation theology as distinct from liberal theology begins not with *any* question, but with Christ as *the* question. . . . Liberation theology is a function of the liberation church." But Herzog contradicts himself. "Theology today," he also affirms, "must begin with an identification with the wretched of the earth, the *marginales,* the marginal figures of life who are still struggling for personhood and dignity."[4] Many of the *marginales* are not Christian, and it is often the gods of the comfortable, dominant, Constantinian church that provide the validation for oppression. We must be careful lest our desire to avoid relativism and to endorse ecclesiastical theology prevent us from joining Jesus Christ "outside the camp" (Heb. 13:13). Pluralism is the complement, not the enemy, of liberation.

Liberation has plural meanings related to differing locations. The oppression from which the Hebrews in ancient Egypt sought deliverance is different from the oppression of serfs in medieval Europe or the oppression of workers caught in the factory system of nineteenth-century industrialism. Oppression takes yet other forms for minorities excluded from equal opportunities in the twentieth century. The hope for liberation is one thing for starving peoples of the Third and Fourth Worlds and quite another for the lonely aging in California convalescent homes. The long march of Exodus is not on the same road for Chinese peasants, for Native Americans, or for women of Western societies. The meaning of liberation shifts with the changing gods that empower human hope and with changing conditions that engender human pain. Most importantly, liberation has different meanings for those who oppress and for those who are oppressed.

These plural meanings for liberation do not weaken

the hope for deliverance or diminish its force. On the contrary, hope calls to hope, and diverse cries of pain strengthen one another. There is power in diversity as well as in unity. The liberating power of pluralism manifests itself in many ways.

First, pluralism can liberate humans from simple location. For many, the place where they were born and reared is the only world they know. At best, existence in such a limited world is impoverished. At worst, it can be a prison in which the prisoners are unaware of their imprisonment. But information about other peoples and other societies can provide a means of liberation. From radio or movies or television, from books about other lands and times, from the Bible, or from stories of heroism and sacrifice, people have found doorways opening into plural worlds that have liberated them from simple location and set their imaginations aflame. The touch of other histories can liberate individuals or whole peoples from the prison of their past. They become aware of the possibilities of liberation, and their simple location exists no more.

Second, pluralism can deliver humans from a constricted circle of limited possibilities and awaken real hope for liberation. One may be aware of other lands and have no hope to visit them. One may peer into the windows of other worlds but never dream of entering them. Other histories, however, speak not only of diverse human locations; they tell also of release from bondage, of movement from slavery toward a promised land of freedom. The story of liberation, especially if told with excitement by the liberated, can kindle expectations that never existed before. Tongue and pen are not only as mighty as the sword; they can give birth to human movements armed with visions and weapons.

Third, pluralism manifests a liberating power by disclosing how widespread is oppression and therefore identifying the possible allies in the struggle for freedom. So long as an oppressed group feels isolated and alone its hopes may burn brightly but remain hidden by a sense of powerlessness. The more a sense of solidarity develops among oppressed groups, the greater becomes their confidence in demanding liberation. Small pockets of workers, isolated in particular factories, could accomplish little. But an organized labor movement under the banner of Solidarity Forever became a powerful economic and political force in the industrial nations. As ethnic minorities and Third World nations discover their common cause of liberation, they will develop alliances as effective as those of the trade and industrial unions.

Fourth, pluralism discloses the varied groups having confidence that a liberating power is at work in many peoples and in reality itself. In spite of economic, political, and theological differences among them, the Judeo-Christian movement, liberal democracy, industrial capitalism, and Marxism all proclaim that the direction of human history is toward liberation. The visions are indeed various among these diverse faiths, but trust in the processes of an encompassing reality is something all of them hold in common. Hope can impel us toward faith in a wholeness of history shaped by liberation. In all these ways, the liberating power of pluralism is made manifest.

James Cone writes, "The task of theology then is to explicate the meaning of God's liberating activity so that those who labor under enslaving powers will see that the forces of liberation are the activity of God."[5] Gayraud Wilmore reminds us that theological transformation is required and underscores the point that liberation cannot be restricted to Christian thought:

Is black theology simply the Blackenization of the whole spectrum of traditional Christian theology, with particular emphasis upon the liberation of the oppressed, or does it find in the experience of the oppression of Black people, as *black*, a singular religiosity, identified not only with Christianity, but with other religions as well?[6]

In Christian faith, what is Christian and what is fully human are never to be totally separated or totally identified, for the pluralism of Hebrew people and Egypt, of Israel and Assyria, of Judah and Babylon, has a place in a larger sovereign reality.

Fifth, pluralism reminds us decisively of the multiple sources and shapes of oppression. Radical evil in history, radical sin in human life, take varied forms. Liberation continues, but new forms of oppression emerge. In part, every liberating achievement opens awareness to new horizons of oppression. In part, the forces of liberation in one generation buttress the oppressor of the next. In part, every movement of liberation is unaware of its own oppressions, such as a labor movement that is oppressive of ethnic minorities and women. Oppression is a hydra-headed monster.

Sixth, pluralism discloses the plurality within liberation itself. Liberation can never be reduced to freedom understood in terms of a single element in the human experience of oppression. There are multiple dimensions to liberation, which must constantly be kept in mind.

Liberation includes deliverance from economic want and oppression. But it also leads toward political freedom and the control of persons over their own destinies in society. Liberation must be seen also in terms of the psychological and cultural freeing of sexual and ethnic groups from the oppression of degradation and projected inferiority. In the same way, nature and humans as natural beings must be included in every complete vision of liberation, as must the freedom to believe and dream toward a more inclusive reality, which is the heart of religious faith and the hope of salvation. Only in terms of pluralism can liberation itself be understood, for any one of these dimensions pursued in isolation from the others would itself be oppressive.[7]

In all these ways, pluralism is a powerful ally of liberation, helping to break the bondage to oppressive structures. The liberation proclaimed by Hebrew prophets, by the community of faith in Jesus Christ, and by many other movements of aspiration and faith that have stirred the hearts and aroused the hopes of humanity has always demanded the courage to embark upon the risks of exodus. In its many forms, pluralism has aided in kindling both vision and courage.

There is another aspect of pluralism important for liberation, one illumined especially by the federal paradigm. The notion of changing gods refers not only to shifting conceptions of deity but also to the liberating power at work in history. One way this power has manifested itself is in the rejection of oppressive gods; that is, in atheism.

2. Faith and the Function of Atheism

Changing gods is more than a matter of diverse faiths shaping human action. When the gods change, it has significance also for the processes of humanizing the world and liberating humanity.

In at least one version of covenant theology, a fascinating alternative to the Augustinian view of creation, fall, and history is suggested. In the Augustinian theology of history, prelapsarian creation is as good as a perfect deity can make it. Humans fall from this created goodness into sin and are redeemed and restored to the lost status in Jesus Christ. This view contains problems that have plagued Western theology, for it appears that there would have been no need for Jesus Christ, no historical function for a Redeemer, if humanity had not fallen. Johannes Cocceius, whose work informs at many points my understanding of federalism, holds that humans are created not at the height of their potential, but mutable, in process toward a consummation hidden in God. Sin means a fall into immutability, into stasis. Redemption means restoration into the creational/historical process toward fulfillment, with Jesus Christ as agent of redemption and consummation whether or not the fall has occurred.[8]

In this federal perspective, nature and history are understood as created *in process,* with successive phases of the covenant of God providing the framework of development. This view may be an important source of various process philosophies in the nineteenth century, particularly those of Hegel and Marx. Though the consummation is shrouded in the future, the covenantal tradition of faith affirms that the sovereign reality of world process is the God of liberation. But the liberating God of one generation becomes the "property" of oppressive social groups in the next generation. For that reason, biblical faith resists the enticing but oppressive idolatry of the past by refusing to give a final name to God. God is revealed in promise and fulfillment, not in one place or era.

God for Christian faith is revealed decisively in Jesus Christ, but Christian theology has been prevented from lapsing into a static Christomonism by the trinitarian faith. God is also Creator, revealed and concealed in natural, historical processes; God is Holy Spirit, bringing all things to an unknown and unimaginable consummation.

There is a pluralism in the God of covenant. The unfolding process of liberation requires multiple and changing gods of human believing in order that the persistent, varied forms of oppression can be overcome. In this way, faith and the function of atheism emerge.

The thought of Ernst Bloch (1885–1977) can be very helpful at this point, especially if absorbed into a covenantal paradigm. Coming out of a German-Jewish background, Bloch had the Hebrew Scriptures as part of his cultural background, even though he never regarded himself as Jewish by faith. His Marxist convictions have had, more than is usual among communists, a strong flavor of social criticism and historical consciousness deriving from the Old Testament. And even in his strangest flights of biblical exegesis there is a core of insight that must not be overlooked.

In *Atheismus im Christentum,* Bloch gives his own reading of the Bible in utopian perspective. The God of traditional religion is always the projection of the unjust social relations of the past extending into the present. This God of an ever-vanishing society of grasping overlords must continually be rejected in favor of utopian ultimacy endowed with the mystery and grandeur of deity. Gods of every social status quo, the gods believed in as the static justification of an unjust order, must be overthrown in favor of the transcending realization of social-historical-utopian consciousness, which takes sides with the oppressed, which leads humans to take history into their own hands and shape it according to their highest dreams.

Bloch's model for revolutionary-utopian humanity is Prometheus, whom Marx calls "the noblest saint in the philosophical calendar," and it is this Promethean paradigm which shapes Bloch's exposition of the Bible. Thus, Bloch says, "only an atheist can be a good Christian"[9]; only someone who defies the gods of the oppressive past can serve the biblical cause of liberation.

This Promethean reading of Scripture reaches its zenith in Jesus, who simultaneously is a militant utopian, a revolutionary, and a rebellious usurper of Yahweh's position. As the son of Man, Jesus exemplifies humanity as ultimate and all-conquering. As son of Man Jesus discloses humanity in total dimensions, as Promethean, as cosmic, and as eschatological power.

Bloch's interpretation offers not so much "an inversion of biblical religion" as a penetrating but inadequate statement of God, humanity, history, and nature in permanent revolution. It is at this point that the covenantal perspective becomes useful. First, because the covenant is so intimately related to biblical religion, it can more easily encompass the varied forms and traditions present there than can the alien myth of Prometheus. Second, the covenant emphasizes rebellion as response to the final power of the universe and as a means to overcome oppression, suggested by Bloch within the Promethean myth. Third, the covenantal perspective suggests the significance of changing gods for the

Hebrew-Christian tradition and for other religious faiths. And fourth, the covenant offers an understanding of plurality, oppression, and change that does not require the pretense of an absolute viewpoint.

In the biblical use of covenants, we see a speaking from faith to faith, which conveys the conviction of reality without the presumption of ascending beyond history to some ontological peak. The most characteristic way of dealing with past and future in the covenantal passages of Scripture is through confession of faith and the recounting of remembered past and anticipated future. Promise and fulfillment provide the fabric of covenantal faith. The God who speaks is heard through the covenant, and the acts through which Yahweh proclaims divine will are historical events received in faith. It is the believed-in God who is confessed and received in covenant. As new events and new insights appear they are absorbed into the interactive pattern of covenant so that the believed-in God is confessed in new and changing ways.

Such a covenantal conception of biblical faith is especially helpful for illumining Bloch's insight into the significance of rebellion and change in relation to socio-political oppression and liberation. The rebellion against the Egyptian oppressors and liberation toward the Promised Land are the occasion for a covenant renewal that redefines the God of Israel at the same time that it redefines the destiny of the People of God. Job's rebellion becomes a dramatic paradigm illustrating a pattern of dwelling in an oppressive conception of deity, protesting against that oppression, and breaking out toward a new conception of deity. In the end God commends Job's rebellion rather than condemning it. Humanity has won a greater measure of liberation, not by a total rejection of deity, but by rebelling against a God of oppression in favor of a more encompassing God of liberation.

The protests of the prophets follow this pattern. The remembered God of the covenant becomes the means for breaking out of oppressive socio-political-theological conditions toward more encompassing liberation and a more comprehensive conception of the covenant God. The dwelling-in of Jesus and his rebellion against the oppressive God of static tradition leads to a breaking-out toward the liberating God who is becoming. Protest leads to death. But death is swallowed up in the resurrection of God and leads humanity toward humanization, liberation, and the making new of all things. Jesus absorbs, reenacts, and alters the covenantal pattern of dwelling-in, rebellion, and breaking-out. The core of Bloch's insight is crucial for an understanding of the dynamism of biblical religion. But the alien myth of Prometheus fails to encompass the wholeness of the human experiencing of God, history, and humanity; a wholeness that the covenantal conception of the Bible itself conveys with greater power.

In this federal perspective, liberation becomes the key to understanding historical change, and Bloch's statement that only an atheist can be a good Christian takes on ever greater significance than he suggests. Only by rebellion against the conceptions of God from the past that are used as instruments of socio-political oppression in the present can we respond to the covenantal call to dwell in and break out. Only in this response can we be faithful to the sovereign God of past, present, and future.

The covenantal paradigm vividly shows the overwhelming importance of changing gods for biblical consciousness and suggests its applicability to the diverse religious consciousness of humanity. Without a decisive concept of change, it is difficult if not impossible to avoid a static notion of deity that fails to encompass the biblical experience of dwelling in and breaking out. Ernst Bloch's reading of the Bible is of great help, not only in illumining the notion of rebelling against God and change in human consciousness, but also in underscoring the dimension of socio-political oppression and the oppressive use of religious tradition. Bloch enables us to see that the process of dwelling in and breaking out is not merely an epistemological exercise, but, because of the indissoluble unity of knowing and acting in human living, it is also bursting the bonds of oppression toward a wider world of human potential and liberation.

The sequential pluralism of covenantal history, with its necessary moments of atheistic rejection of deities used for purposes of oppression, is as essential for liberation as is the contemporary pluralism of diverse communities of interpretation. Liberation becomes the key for discerning the pattern of change in pluralism, tracing the meaning of theological transformation, and delineating appropriate human responses to change.

3. Theological Tents and Imperial Palaces

If it becomes necessary to make a choice of dwelling places for the intellect, H. Richard Niebuhr once remarked, he would be compelled to choose a tent. For humanity on the journey of life in a changing world, Niebuhr's selection is apt. The most appropriate habitation for those who would understand human believing from locations in transit will always be a theological tent rather than an imperial palace.

Those who fear the impact of change on conventional theology are correct about its dangers. The problem, however, is not with change itself or with theology. Cultural and social change constitute a peril only for theologies built upon static concepts or chained to the formulations of a "classical" past. Historical currents gradually undermine and topple immobile theological domiciles.

Recognition of the significance of change for religious faith does not mean rejection of the past. It does mean refusing to become enslaved to what has gone before. Whitehead speaks for the Judeo-Christian tradition and probably for all vital forms of human believing when he says, "Idolatry is the necessary product of static dogmas."[10] Instead, humanity immersed in the sovereign reality of world process dwells in the past in order to break out toward the future. In change we confront God as the not-yet, and so are driven to seek deity as much in the emerging unknown, in the anticipation of the new, as in the covenants of tradition that have shaped us.

Within a federal paradigm for theology, continuity and change are complementary to one another. So also are pluralism and liberation. When liberation becomes a central motif of theology, the crucial contribution of pluralism in disclosing and overcoming oppression appears. In parallel fashion, the power of atheism in exposing the idolatrous gods of socio-political oppressors clearly becomes the necessary complement to faith in the liberating God of covenant.

A theological tent rather than an imperial palace is necessary as the abode of those who take the covenantal perspective seriously. When creation and history are in process, human believing and reflection responsive to reality must be on the move. Theologians today are being evicted from the imperial palace provided by the Constantinian paradigm and compelled, usually against their will, to dwell again in tents.

As the traditional pattern of Christian theology fades, we must learn again lessons obvious to that tentmaker, the apostle Paul. No longer can the dominance of organized Christianity be assumed and concepts of God and religion be drawn from that one tradition. The scope of theology cannot be limited to the Christian theology of the North Atlantic academies. Theology can no longer be restricted to a particular ecclesiastical enclave but must be enlarged to take account of global pluralism and liberation. In similar fashion theology need no longer be dependent upon one or another philosophy either in method or style. Linguistic philosophy, Whitehead, Hartshorne, Heidegger—none is forbidden, but neither does any one of these offer the "right philosophy" or the necessary method for theology. The attention of theology is on the patterns of commitments governing the wholeness of experiencing and action rather than only on rational criteria and symbol systems. And, of course, theologians are being forced to relinquish the imperial mood as the Constantinian paradigm dissolves.

Learning to dwell in theological tents, as did our Hebrew forebears and many Christians in lands beyond the sway of Constantine, is a difficult task for theologians. It requires openness to the power of transformation. Most difficult, perhaps, is learning to admit without embarrassment our human location. We dwell within a wholeness of experiencing that provides us with possibilities even as it defines our limits. Our believing points to the horizons and to the shaping commitments of our location. Our knowing takes place within the perspective, presuppositions, and fiduciary context of covenantal wholeness.

Within human location, theology and ethics are distinguishable but inseparable. The sovereign reality of human believing is a center of value shaping the ethics of a community. But the value structure of human interaction provides the fiduciary validation of believed-in deities. God as reality and value, humans in their believing, and the patterns of communal commitment and action form a triad in which there is no theology apart from ethics or ethics apart from theology.

Dwelling in tents reminds theologians that human living is grounded in faith. Attempts to reduce faith to a form of knowledge are no longer possible. And the view that knowing escapes a comprehensive context with fiduciary foundations is exposed as illusory.

For Christians, this reminder is helpful. It aids in resisting the temptations to substitute an absolutized church or morality or traditional dogma for the triune God of covenant. Christians are opened to the recognition of the partial character of human believing and made receptive to *metanoia,* to "permanent revolution," that continues beyond particular locations, times, and formulations.

In this perspective, creation is not left as "a protological myth of origin, but as an eschatological 'project,' " as

Gerhard Sauter puts it.[11] Liberation and revolution are not events in the past but continuing and ongoing processes built into human history and empowering the continuing revolution of divine purpose.

When theology dwells in tents rather than in palaces, we are able to see the plural, changing gods of human believing and recognize this pluralism as ground of hope. Biblical religion is rooted in the expectation of change, in the new, in hope. It declares an end to static metaphysics, to satisfaction with the present, to possibility limited by present horizons. Reality is in process toward unthinkable possibilities of which we are dimly aware through hope. God is perceived in the mystery of the future as well as in the multiplicity of contemporary deities. Only a theology which can distinguish and operate with changing deities, the deities of other communities as well as the God and gods of the theologian's own location, is capable of anticipating the future and comprehending social change. When we are open toward the God who is becoming, we are prepared to believe and act in hope.

But this hope is not to be interpreted only in individual terms or as the expectation of some distant consummation. Rather it must be seen as hope for concrete possibilities *now* for a more humane society in a healthy natural order. This is the hope of the ethnic minority for economic and political justice. It is the hope of women to overcome oppression. It is the hope of humanity for the cessation of war and the establishment of peace. It is the hope that we can stop the pollution of our planet and learn to treat it with the respect owed to the created order.

The nomadic setting of a tent liberates theology from bondage to rationalism. Without rejecting the fruits of technology and the Western intellectual tradition, theologians can appreciate again the power of story, saga, and parable for theological style and recognize again the importance of ritual and tradition for human believing. The encompassing fiduciary dimensions of communities of interpretation must be expressed in story, image, and root metaphor. Language and reason operate within the horizons of tradition and faith; the more discursive and rational the language, the less adequate it is to express the most comprehensive commitments of human living.

In this way, the theological tents of covenantal faith restore a sense of mystery of historical location. Yet the mystery does not produce a sense of lostness but rather a sense of possibilities hidden within the future.

Faith in this mysterious reality that appears when gods change pulls us into a widening future. The most sovereign power of our experiencing as Christians is God not only of our history, of Hebrew-Christian history, but of all human histories. In choosing us, God chooses all humanity. The old tension in Hebrew faith between the exclusiveness of our limited loyalty and the inclusiveness of God's unlimited love remains. We live by what we have learned from our ancestors, but we hope also to learn of God from all humans. We do not relinquish the heritage of our faith, but we understand it through the expanding experience of global relationships. We live toward a future that includes the histories of all communities and in which the world is the homeland of all peoples.

We speak then of changing gods, some dying and others being born. We speak also of the resurrection of the gods as the histories they represent are transmuted into more comprehensive histories. The causes and loyalties to which humans give themselves die in the narrow forms given them by human believing but have a place in resurrected, changed form within a reality beyond the widest dreams of our future consciousness. Into this nomadic life of dwelling in theological tents, toward this vision of God beyond our visions, global pluralism and liberation call the human communities of interpretation and faith as the gods change.

CODA

STANDING IN AN APERTURE

To believe in something not yet proved and to underwrite it with our lives; it is the only way we can leave the future open. Humanity, surrounded by facts, permitting itself no surmise, no intuitive flash, no great hypothesis, no risk is in a locked cell. Ignorance cannot seal the mind and imagination more surely. To find the point where hypothesis and fact meet; the delicate equilibrium between dream and reality; the place where fantasy and earthly things are metamorphosed into a work of art; the hour when faith in the future becomes knowledge of the past; to lay down one's power for others in need; to shake off the old ordeal and get ready for the new; to question, knowing that never can the full answer be found; to accept uncertainties quietly, even our incomplete knowledge of God: this is what the human journey is about . . .

Lillian Smith, The Journey

XII.

A FUTURE
FOR THEOLOGY
AND ETHICS

"The world is full of stale religion," observed Walter Rauschenbush. "It is historically self-evident that church bodies . . . may become social agencies to keep their people stupid, stationary, superstitious, bigoted, and ready to choke their first-born ideals and instincts as a sacrifice to the God of stationariness."[1] The world is also full of stale theology and ethics, devoted to static deities and oppressive moralism.

But another power is at work. "A broad and deep aspiration for liberation inflames the history of humankind, in our day," writes Gustavo Gutierrez. "Liberation from all that limits or keeps humanity from self-fulfillment, liberation from all impediments to the exercise of human freedom."[2] Slowly and with much suffering, the power of liberation overcomes oppressive social structures and stale religion.

Movements of liberation were not created by Berkeley students in the sixties or by Third World revolutionaries. Nor is the theology of liberation a product only of the seventies. It would be a profound act of injustice and ingratitude on our part if we were to forget the movements in our own past whose beneficiaries we are—the civil rights movement, the courageous fighters for women's suffrage, the labor movement, the social

226

gospel, the anti-slavery movement, and the American Revolution. And it is no less an injustice to overlook the suffering and the achievements of those who have worked for human rights in every land and on every continent. As human beings, we are a part of a long march out of the lands of bondage.

To experience this exodus, today or in any present, is to come alive to possibilities hidden within the future. Awakened to a world in midpassage, we remember the time of bondage and anticipate the promised time of liberation. We know ourselves to be standing in a great historic aperture, looking backward toward the old and forward toward emerging newness.

Theology and ethics in Europe and North America are, in this perspective, also on the way of exodus. Religious faith and reflection are moving out of their traditional bondage to ecclesiastical and academic enclaves, through the wilderness of global culture with its strange sights and diverse deities, toward patterns of renewal and hope. In theology and ethics, we are standing in an aperture.

Imprisoned within the Constantinian paradigm, theology is sick, verging on exhaustion. But theology is no more dead than is the sovereign reality toward which it points. Theology instead is in the process of transformation. The traditional pattern of Western theology, rather than shifting to a "new key,"[3] is dissolving, and a new paradigm is evolving. In spite of predictions of demise, theology will continue, but not in the forms most prevalent today. Theology and ethics have a future, but only when static forms give way to transformation. When gods change, there is hope for theology.

The past demonstrates that fundamental theological change is possible. Indeed, the Constantinian paradigm itself emerged as the result of such alteration. In view of the rapidly shifting conditions of society in this century, it should occasion no surprise that a revolution of major proportions is taking place in Christian theology.

WHEN GODS CHANGE

1. Transformation as Fulfillment

The federal paradigm, I believe, provides a shape and method for transformed theology, a means for comprehending pluralism and liberation in their global scope. It remains faithful to the Judeo-Christian heritage in its full dimensions of promise and fulfillment. Covenantal theology and ethics, with this paradigm, can meet the challenge of contemporary cultural change while maintaining continuity with the past.

To put it even more strongly, this transformed theology may prove to be more of a fulfillment of our biblical heritage than were the Constantinian theologies now turned stale. Far too easily, "traditions become the epitome of inherited prejudice"[4] and the vehicles of oppression. The prophetic and messianic passions of biblical faith, as Moltmann has reminded us, are eschatological at their heart, oriented toward the future, toward fulfillment, toward freedom. The close kinship between that radical faith and the revolution of rising expectations and the global diversity of our time may be overlooked in favor of stale and dying traditions. Trying to remain in a static past, rather than being faithful to our heritage, becomes the most total betrayal of the promise of that heritage.

Covenantal faith also provides a means for being faithful to another aspect of the exodus heritage and its counterpart in Christianity: "Therefore let us go forth to him outside the camp, bearing abuse for him. For here we have no lasting city, but we seek the city which is to come" (Heb. 13:13-14). We are not faithful to the God of Abraham and Sarah if we remain complacently in the location of our birth and refuse the call to journey forth in faith to seek the promised homeland. We are not faithful to the God of Moses, the God whose identity is given in the words, "I am becoming who I am becoming" (Exod. 3:14), if we prefer the fleshpots of secure churchly affluence to the long march of covenant liberation. It is no evidence of faithfulness to the crucified Jesus Christ to adhere to ecclesiastical tradition rather than risk involvement with a troubled world outside the camp. Judeo-Christian faith is a movement continually in exodus, moving toward a future informed and empowered by the promise embodied in the past.

Martin Buber finds in Amos 9:7 "between the lines, that by whatever name this or that people call their historic liberator god, all such gods are one, one whose true name has been entrusted to Israel."[5] When gods change, therefore, they continue pointing to the sovereign reality that the prophets proclaimed as revolutionizing consciousness, action, and history. Theology liberated from bondage to the gods of the past is prepared to aid humanity to move through the aperture of this present toward that liberating power that makes all things new. In this way, theology participates in change and liberation.

Transformed theology offers us guidance in meeting the challenge of Marxism. Religion becomes an opiate only when it is stale, when it falls captive to oppressive social powers. "The religious misery," Karl Marx wrote, "is at once the expression of the real misery and the protest against the real misery."[6] When theology and ethics reflect that real misery, participate in it, and join the protest against it, they stimulate response to that power of liberation at work in human misery.

In his famous thesis in criticism of Feuerbach, Marx said: "The philosophers have only interpreted the world, in various ways; the point, however, is to *change* it." Here, as at many other points, Marxism discloses its religious intentions, that is, to be believing action rather than intellectual analysis remote from human misery. Theology transformed by movements of pluralism and liberation deals inescapably with action and change, not with reflection alone. And further, to the extent that persons in theology and ethics recognize their location as religious, they become conscious participants in human misery and the struggle for deliverance.

Even as we learn from Marxism, we must be wary of it.

229

It is not Marxist theology that awaits us on the other side of the aperture through which we are now passing. The theory of Marxism often resembles in unhappy ways the ecclesiastical theologies we are leaving behind.

First, intellectuals of Marxist persuasion, including Marx himself, have frequently been more interested in intellectual interpretation than in action on behalf of liberation. Whether we call them armchair Marxists or persons who, like many Christians, spend their time repenting of the sins of others rather than their own, those who profess Marxist theology and ethics cannot be regarded as unequivocally reliable guides toward the future.

Second, I have difficulty with the dictum of Marx against Feuerbach, not in its emphasis on changing the world, but with its implication that it is possible to change the world without understanding it. Viewing the suffering of humanity at a distance, understanding it only for the sake of analytic accuracy, fits no better with the exodus faith of the Hebrew prophets, with Christian faith in the crucified God, or with many another faith informed by liberation, than it fits with the intention of Marxist faith. Attempts to change the world that hope to reach beyond futile gestures must combine prophetic passion, expert inquiry, and skillful capabilities for the effective alteration of social structures. In this perspective, a transformed theology can play a crucial role in human liberation by combining analysis and change.

Third, theology on the other side of the aperture will seek for a greater wholeness of human freedom and humanity than Marxist theology usually provides. A federal paradigm suggests the multiple dimensions that must be taken into account in the process of human liberation. Humans are economic beings in need of liberation from oppressive forces that prevent securing food, clothing, shelter, and livelihood. But humanity is more than economic. Humans are political—in need of liberation from bondage to the state and all powers that prevent a voice in the control of social structures.

Humans are ethnic, sexual, and cultural beings. Humans are psychological, expressive beings, who strive for freedom in terms of dignity and sense of self-worth. Cultural and psychological violence and oppression can be as cruel as outright physical torture. Humans are also children of nature, in need of ecological awareness. And humans are religious beings, and there is no more serious infringement of freedom than alienation from meaning and the oppressive absence of channels to express the depths of human believing. Marxist social analysis, as well as societies shaped by Marxist faith, often seem thin, one-dimensional, in their understanding of human living and liberation—no less than the sectors of bourgeois society that are insensitive to the larger dimensions of what it means to be human.

2. Revolution as Historical Process

Theologians of the North Atlantic academies who become concerned about the stark oppressions of the world today often arrive at the conviction that revolution is preferable to the slow strategies of reform. Few, however, explore the differing meanings of revolution and, consequently, assume that violent revolution is the only alternative to gradualism. The perspective of a transformed theology throws interesting light on revolution, a term often treated as a fad rather than used to designate political or theological change.

Though some political philosophers regard violence as "an irreducible element of any revolution,"[7] Guenther Lewy's view is historically more adequate. "Revolution is an abrupt, though not necessarily violent, change in the political system, including the nature of rulership or constitution and the principles of legitimacy upon which these rest."[8] This understanding permits us to see the differing relations of religious tradition and political revolution, but it is not sufficiently broad for cultural and theological purposes.

In the broadest sense, there have been two revolutionary political movements over the past half millennium. The first of these is the middle-class revolution, which swept out of western Europe in the sixteenth century and around the globe in the years since. The second is the proletarian revolution, which emerged in the nineteenth century and has commanded the loyalties of many groups excluded from the benefits of the middle-class revolution.

Though Constantinian religion has supported existing social orders, Christianity has continued to spawn movements that have sought social change and have sometimes been revolutionary. Thomas Münzer, for example, represents the revolutionary potentialities of the left wing of the Reformation. Of even greater importance has been the revolutionary impact of the Reformed tradition. In Switzerland, in parts of Germany, in the Netherlands, in Scotland, in England, and in the British colonies in America, the Reformed movement was the spearhead of the middle-class revolution in all its dimensions—political, economic, social, psychological, scientific, and technological.

In political life, the middle-class revolution involved the shift of power from kings and nobility to the rising commercial classes. Zürich, Geneva, and Bremen exemplify this revolution in Switzerland and Germany. The Dutch Republic illustrates the creative, expansionist power of the bourgeois revolution at its most explosive. The National Covenant in Scotland and the Puritans under Cromwell represent the movement in Britain: in the Roundhead armies "even cobblers and tinkers" were encouraged to participate in political discussion and action. Puritan politics was transported to America, shaped the governments of the British colonies, and eventuated in the American Revolution and the Federal Constitution. Republican government with strong democratizing tendencies developed under the impact of the middle-class revolution.

The economic, scientific, technological, and industrial

components of the bourgeois revolution have been as important and as striking as the political changes. Europe, scarcely more than a musty corner of a larger world in the Middle Ages, emerged as the most powerful force on the world's scene, and by the opening of the twentieth century dominated the globe. The United States, with its continental space and vast resources, inherited this revolution from Europe and has succeeded to much of its power.

The bourgeois revolution is without doubt among the most powerful social upheavals of human history. It liberated millions and developed structures to protect them. But it also resulted in new patterns of oppression. By 1976, over two-thirds of the globe's four billion inhabitants could be numbered among the poor and oppressed. Even so, the middle-class revolution produced the rising tide of expectations around the world, which provided the impetus for the proletarian revolution.

Two elements permeate the federalism of the bourgeois movement: first, the conviction that humanity individually and collectively is in midpassage toward a higher and as yet undisclosed liberation and consummation; second, the conviction that pluralism will serve the cause of human liberation. The middle-class revolution is based firmly on belief in liberation and the liberating power of pluralism.

The roots of proletarian revolution are to be found in the ill-starred rebellions of serfs and slaves since time immemorial. But the impetus from the bourgeois revolution and the partial liberation it brought provided the setting for Marxist teaching and for a powerful Marxist movement. The prophetic fervor for justice of the Judeo-Christian movement informed Marxism even as Marxists rejected the theology that had become at least partly a tool of oppressor groups.

Against the economic, political, and ecclesiastical power of the bourgeoisie, Marxism called for the development of highly centralized movements aimed at overthrowing liberal democracies and establishing dictatorships of the proletariat. The middle-class governments proved too strong to overthrow, though they could be penetrated and influenced. Not in western Europe, where it developed amid the industrial exploitation at which it was aimed, but in the agrarian lands of Russia and China, did Marxism have its greatest successes.

The accomplishments of the proletarian revolution, no less than those of the bourgeois revolution, ought not to be underestimated. It overcame oppressive systems of government and brought impressive measures of economic and political liberation to millions of oppressed people in eastern Europe and Asia. In addition, millions more around the globe who had become disillusioned with the increasingly oppressive character of bourgeois society now found hope.

The problems of this revolutionary movement also must not be underestimated. Whereas bourgeois societies have a built-in pluralism which compels reform and revolution to continue, the proletarian dictatorships produce impressive results quickly but then tend to harden at the level of liberation attained. The state does not wither away. Permanent revolution proves impermanent. A major reason is that the liberating power of pluralism in communist states is virtually eliminated. The centralized power that insured the initial step of liberation tends to eliminate the diversity of views that are crucial for continuing liberation.

From the standpoint of commitment to human liberation, it has been an error of the first magnitude to assume that the bourgeois and proletarian revolutions are inevitably opposed. Rather than seeing them only through the enmity represented in opposing political movements and nation-states, and believing it necessary to choose one to the exclusion of the other, it becomes increasingly clear that it is essential to choose both and use elements from each. The liberating power of pluralism built into the middle-class revolution and the creativity that pluralism engenders must be joined to the egalitarian spirit of the proletarian revolution and to the determination that has informed its intentions to extend liberation to the poorest and the weakest.

These forms of revolution do not exhaust its meaning. There are also the cultural and spiritual revolutions of consciousness that change patterns of human interaction no less than do political revolutions.

The impact of Jesus and the gospel illustrates this latter meaning of revolution. Take, for example, his attitude toward women, viewed especially against the background of the status of women in the Judaism of that time. Writes Elisabeth Moltmann-Wendel: "He encountered women as well as men with complete naturalness and spontaneous matter-of-factness. . . . It is true that he never demanded emancipation, just as he never called for a social revolution. But his speech and his life contain a kind of dynamite which could one day erase social barriers and the separation of the sexes."[9]

Movements by Mahatma Gandhi and Martin Luther King, Jr., are further illustrations of cultural and spiritual revolution. In a paraphrase of a statement from Gandhi, King describes this revolutionary method in language reflecting theological transformation:

We shall match your capacity to inflict suffering by our capacity to endure suffering. We will meet your physical force with soul force. Do to us what you will and we will still love you. We cannot in all good conscience obey your unjust laws and abide by the unjust system, because noncooperation with evil is as much a moral obligation as is cooperation with good, and so throw us in jail and we will still love you. Bomb our homes and threaten our children, and, as difficult as it is, we will still love you. Send your hooded perpetrators of violence into our communities at the midnight hour and drag us out on some wayside road and leave us half-dead as you beat us, and we will still love you. Send your propaganda agents around the country, and make it appear that we are not fit, culturally and otherwise, for integration, and we'll still love you. But be assured that we'll wear you down by our capacity to suffer, and one day we will win our freedom. We will not only win freedom for ourselves; we will so appeal to your heart and conscience that we will win you in the process, and our victory will be a double victory.[10]

Still a further meaning refers to what H. Richard Niebuhr calls "permanent revolution." What he points to with his phrase is genuine revolution. It is not rooted in human initiative alone, though it changes human purpose, action, and social structures decisively. The basis of this revolution is the sovereign power at work in history and nature. I have appealed to this believed-in reality in my discussions of liberation. Whether explicitly or not, political appeals for change, Marxist and all, assume a sovereign reality supporting, reinforcing, and assuring that fulfilling change will indeed take place. Transformation in theology throws considerable light on the varied meanings of revolution and historical process.

3. Liberation as Human Destiny

Within the federal paradigm, theologians can rediscover the contributions theology and ethics make in illumining the religious dimensions of the human condition. Transformed theology will not be detached from particular communities of faith. It seems clear that leaving all human location is impossible. The scope of its attention and methods, however, will not be limited to a single community. Even when articulating the convictions of their own community, theologians will take into account the theological work of other communities. As theologians of many persuasions become actively engaged in ecumenical, intercommunal exchange and joint endeavor, their work will not only better serve their own groups but will also once again show the relation of human believing to all the processes of society and to the continuing thrust of liberation.

Theology and theologians, even on the wider basis proposed here, cannot work in isolation from other academic disciplines. Indeed, the transformation of theology points the way toward the return of theology into the university and societal context from which Constantinian theology in its more ecclesiastical manifestations withdrew. Changing human action requires understanding the full range of the goals and means of that action. Theology, wrestling with human issues of religious believing and action, has a necessary part to play in such an understanding—along with political science, history, sociology, psychology, economics, the arts, and so on. Wholeness of understanding is a cross-disciplinary undertaking, in which the entire spectrum of studies has a crucial role to play. The way of transformation for theology is the way of renewal as a university discipline.

The hope of making changes of a genuinely liberating nature in our complex society, however, requires more than academic and interdisciplinary efforts. Effective, enduring, and continuing change means the combining of commitment, expertise, and power. Liberation requires a triadic approach: the understanding and skills of persons from theology and ethics to disclose the patterns of human commitment, the expertise of social, biological, and physical scientists relevant for particular spheres of suffering and oppression, and the insight and power of persons occupying positions in the arenas of decision and policy (those who are the recipients of policy as well as those who shape it). No less inclusive alliances than these can serve well the cause of human liberation.

The federal paradigm provides the means to understand the plurality of religious, political, and social commitment present on the global scene. The constellations of meaning and power that must be reckoned with today can best be delineated in terms of the multiple and shifting deities shaping culture and producing the valencies governing human action systems. What can be discerned on a global scale can also be discovered on the national level and in the action systems of smaller social units. By investigating what God or gods are the operative centers of valuing for this state, for that city, in this ecclesiastical structure, in that political organization or local parish, it becomes possible to understand with considerable precision the interests and purposes that govern the political, economic, and religious action around us. To grasp the theological shape of social entities in this way enables us to comprehend better the dynamics of societal life, the changes taking place around us, and the strategies of liberation.

When all that we can do is done, however, we must remember that we rely not on human energies alone but on a sovereign power at work in the reality of historical process, a power making for liberation—"new every morning; great in faithfulness" (Lam. 3:23). And strange as it may seem, when we commit our lives to that sovereign reality we experience a surge of power greater than our own efforts, greater even than the synergistic power experienced in community. From his confessional stance as Christian, Niebuhr describes this experience of faith. "We sought a good to love and were found by a good that loved us. And therewith all our religious ambitions are brought low, all our desire to be ministers of God are humbled; God is our minister."[11]

Though faith in the God of covenant focuses our attention on the emerging wholeness of grace, we must remember the presence of continuing, stubborn resistance to good. Evil is real and takes ever-new forms in the history of reluctant liberation. No theological paradigm embodying Hebrew-Christian faith can encourage naïve optimism about human possibilities in all their mixed ambiguities. The Holocaust and Hiroshima are as real as Dietrich Bonhoeffer and the Marshall Plan. Changing gods, the widening horizons of good and evil, the arrival of ever-new futures are not without trauma. But trauma and catastrophe, understood in covenant faith, lead through pain toward liberation. In the frenzy of affluence, in fascination with trivia, we forget that the path toward freedom is by way of the cross and resurrection. It is an exodus history, this story of our lives, this life in Jesus Christ. We live, as Michael Polanyi and Jürgen Moltmann remind us, through faith in "the crucified God."

A FUTURE FOR THEOLOGY AND ETHICS

Closer than mere optimism to the biblical under-standing of the terrible and glorious possibilities hidden within the onrushing torrent of human experi-ence are these passages from William Styron's *Set This House on Fire:*

> What this great land of ours needs is something to happen to it. Something ferocious and tragic, like what happened to Jericho or the cities of the plain—something terrible . . . so that when the people have been through hellfire and the crucible, and have suffered agony enough and grief, they'll be . . . human beings, not a bunch of smug contented hogs rooting at the trough.

Yet at the end there is hope:

> Now I suppose I should tell you that through some sort of suffering I had reached grace . . . that I had found some belief, some rock, and that here on this rock anything might prevail . . . even death itself no longer, but a resurrection.
>
> But to be truthful, I can only tell you this: that as for being and nothingness, the one thing I did know was that to choose between them was simply to choose being, not for the sake of being, or even for the love of being, much less the desire to be forever—but in the hope of being what I could be for a time. This would be an ecstasy. God knows, it would.

As Styron perceives, our being as humans is never without turmoil, and never on rocklike solidity, but rather is becoming in time, in the real particularities of human location. A home for humanity, therefore, will always be a tent, set up along the human journey to provide modest shelter from the storms of living.

Change shatters our comfort and our gods. But the trauma, as it destroys static dogmas and stationary deities, is the preparation for a future filled with greater justice, freedom, human inclusiveness, and even love, made possible when gods change.

Standing in an aperture, we find pluralism not a peril but a force empowering the future. When gods change there is hope for theology, and for humanity. Our faith is in that sovereign reality at work in us and around us—liberating us from outmoded faiths and oppressive deities, liberating us for the fulfillment of our human destiny in God.

NOTES

Chapter 2: Theology in Transformation

1. Jürgen Moltmann, Introduction to Ernst Bloch, *Man on His Own: Essays in the Philosophy of Religion* (New York: Herder and Herder, 1970), p. 26.

2. James William McClendon, Jr., *Biography as Theology: How Life Stories Can Remake Today's Theology* (Nashville: Abingdon Press, 1974), p. 13.

3. Rosemary Radford Ruether, *Liberation Theology: Human Hope Confronts Christian History and American Power* (New York: Paulist Press, 1972), p. 2.

4. Rudolf Bultmann, *History and Eschatology: The Presence of Eternity* (New York: Harper Torchbooks, 1962), pp. 129, 154.

5. Jürgen Moltmann, *Theology of Hope: On the Ground and Implications of a Christian Eschatology* (New York: Harper & Row, 1967), pp. 16, 26; altered slightly to avoid sexist language.

6. H. Richard Niebuhr, *The Meaning of Revelation* (New York: The Macmillan Co., 1941), pp. viii-ix.

7. *Ibid.,* pp. 46-47.

Chapter 3: Pluralism as Problem and Possibility

1. William James, *A Pluralistic Universe* (New York: Longmans, Green, 1909), pp. 321-22.

2. Bertrand Russell, *The Scientific Outlook* (New York: W. W. Norton & Co., 1931), p. 98.

3. See Helmut Spinner, *Pluralismus als Erkenntnismodell* (Frankfurt a.M.: Suhrkamp Verlag, 1974), *passim.*

4. Harvey Cox, *The Seduction of the Spirit: The Use and Misuse of People's Religion* (New York: Simon & Schuster, 1973), p. 318.

5. George W. Forell, *The Proclamation of the Gospel in a Pluralistic World: Essays on Christianity and Culture* (Philadelphia: Fortress Press, 1973), p. 2.

6. H. Richard Niebuhr, *The Purpose of the Church and Its Ministry* (New York: Harper and Brothers, 1956), p. 3.

Chapter 4: Reappearance of the Gods

1. Eberhard Jüngel, *Gott als Geheimnis der Welt. Zur Begründung der Theologie des Gekreuzigten im Streit zwischen Theismus und Atheismus* (Tübingen: J. C. B. Mohr [Paul Siebeck], 1977²), S. 1 ff.

2. Thomas Luckmann, *The Invisible Religion: The Problem of Religion in Modern Society* (New York: The Macmillan Co., 1967), pp. 22-24, 28-40.

3. Michael Novak, *Belief and Unbelief: A Philosophy of Self-Knowledge* (New York: The Macmillan Co., 1966); Gerhard Ebeling, *The Nature of Faith* (London: Collins Fontana, 1966), pp. 20-21. See also M. C. d'Arcy, *The Nature of Belief* (London: Sheed & Ward, 1931); Martin Marty, *Varieties of Unbelief* (New York: Holt, Rinehart and Winston, 1964); and Kai Nielsen, *Contemporary Critiques of Religion* (New York: The Macmillan Co., 1971).

4. Karl Barth, *Evangelical Theology: An Introduction* (New York: Holt, Rinehart and Winston, 1963), pp. 3-4.

5. Ernst Benz, *Neue Religionen* (Stuttgart: Ernst Klett Verlag, 1971), S. 7-8.

6. Ninian Smart, *The Religious Experience of Mankind* (New York: Charles Scribner's Sons, 1969), p. 518.

7. Robert Bellah, *Beyond Belief: Essays on Religion in a Post-Traditional World* (New York: Harper & Row, 1970), p. 223.

8. Concerning Japan, see the book with a title which might well describe the religious situation in the world today, H. N. McFarland, *The Rush Hour of the Gods: A Study of New Religious Movements in Japan* (New York: The Macmillan Co., 1967).

9. See J. Stilson Judah, *A History of the Metaphysical Movements* (Philadelphia: The Westminster Press, 1967).

10. See Frederick Sontag, *Sun Yung Moon and the Unification Church* (Nashville: Abingdon, 1977).

11. Thomas F. Torrance, *Theological Science* (London: Oxford University Press, 1969), p. 264.

12. *Ibid.*, pp. 7, 9, 325, viii-ix, x.

13. Bernard J. F. Lonergan, S.J., *Method in Theology* (New York: Herder and Herder, 1972), p. 4.

14. *Ibid.*, pp. 279-80.

15. *Ibid.*, pp. 353, 101, 326 and elsewhere.

16. David Tracy, *Blessed Rage for Order: The New Pluralism in Theology* (New York: The Seabury Press, 1975), p. 3.

17. John Cobb, *Christ in a Pluralistic Age* (Philadelphia: The Westminster Press, 1975), pp. 21, 60, 187. Space does not permit treatment of the relation between process theology based upon a covenantal or federal perspective and process theology based upon twentieth-century philosophy, and the probable historical derivation of

the latter from the former. That discussion must be reserved for another time.

Chapter 5: The Mystery of Location

1. See, for example, the notion of *participation mystique* in L. Lévy-Bruhl, *Primitive Mentality* (London: G. Allen and Unwin, 1923); and *How Natives Think* (London: G. Allen and Unwin, 1926).

2. See J. Piaget, *The Child's Conception of Physical Causality* (London: Kegan Paul, 1930); and *The Construction of Reality in the Child* (New York: Basic Books, 1954).

3. For illustrations with their epistemological implications and significance, see the impressive work of Michael Polanyi, in particular *Personal Knowledge: Towards a Post-Critical Philosophy* (Chicago: University of Chicago Press, 1958); and *The Tacit Dimension* (Garden City, N.Y.: Doubleday & Co., 1966).

4. John Macmurray, *The Self as Agent* (London: Faber & Faber, 1957), p. 12.

5. *The Social Psychology of George Herbert Mead*, ed. Anselm Strauss (Chicago: University of Chicago Press, 1956), p. 112.

6. Margaret Ribble, *The Rights of Infants* (New York: Columbia University Press, 1943).

7. Rollo May, *Love and Will* (New York: W. W. Norton & Co., 1969), p. 19.

8. Polanyi, *Personal Knowledge*, p. 112.

9. Herbert W. Richardson, *Toward an American Theology* (New York: Harper & Row, 1967), p. 68.

10. H. Richard Niebuhr, *The Meaning of Revelation*, p. 80.

Chapter 6: The Dis-ease of Western Theology

1. H. Richard Niebuhr, *The Meaning of Revelation*, p. 43.

2. *The Stromata*, VI, 10, 18. The Ante-Nicene Fathers, Vol. II (Buffalo, 1885), pp. 498, 519.

3. Gerhard Ebeling, *Das Wesen des christlichen Glaubens* (München und Hamburg: Siebenstern Taschenbuch Verlag, 1964), S. 14.

4. Peter L. Berger, Brigitte Berger, Hansfried Kellner, *The Homeless Mind: Modernization and Consciousness* (New York: Random House, 1973), pp. 64, 80.

5. Walter Rauschenbusch, *Christianity and the Social Crisis* (New York: The Macmillan Co., 1907), p. 46.

6. On this anomaly, see A. O. Lovejoy, *The Great Chain of Being* (Cambridge, Mass: Harvard University Press, 1936), p. 5.

7. Richard R. Niebuhr, *Resurrection and Historical Reason: A Study of Theological Method* (New York: Charles Scribner's Sons, 1957), pp. 80-81.

8. John A. T. Robinson, *Honest to God* (London: SCM Press, 1963), p. 7.

9. Harvey Cox, *The Secular City* (New York: The Macmillan Co., 1965), pp. 2, 106, 107, 197.

10. Paul van Buren, *The Secular Meaning of the Gospel* (New York: The Macmillan Co., 1963), pp. xiii, 20, 100, 197.

11. Gabriel Vahanian, "Swallowed Up by Godlessness," *The Christian Century*, December 8, 1965, p. 1507.

12. Joseph Fletcher, "The New Look in Christian Ethics," *Harvard Divinity Bulletin*, October, 1959, p. 10.

13. Joseph Fletcher, *Situation Ethics: The New Morality* (Philadelphia: The Westminster Press, 1966). See also John A. T. Robinson, *Christian Morals Today* (Philadelphia: The Westminster Press, 1964).

14. John Rawls, *A Theory of Justice* (Cambridge, Mass: Belknap Press, 1971); and Kai Nielsen, *Ethics Without God* (London: Pemberton Books, 1973).

15. See David Miller, *The New Polytheism* (New York: Harper & Row, 1974); William Hamilton, *On Taking God Out of the Dictionary* (New York: McGraw-Hill, 1974); John Y. Fenton, ed., *Theology and Body* (Philadelphia: The Westminster Press, 1974); Tom F. Driver, *Patterns of Grace* (New York: Harper & Row, 1977); and Thomas C. Oden, *Agenda for Theology* (New York: Harper & Row, 1979).

Chapter 7: Religion and Change

1. Mircea Eliade, *The Sacred and the Profane* (New York: Harper Torchbook, 1961), p. 92.

2. Berger, *et al., The Homeless Mind,* pp. 64, 80, 82.

3. Daniel Bell, *The Cultural Contradictions of Capitalism* (New York: Basic Books, 1976), pp. 29, 30.

4. William James, *Pragmatism* (New York: Longmans, Green, 1907), p. 260.

5. José Pintauro and Sister Corita, *To Believe in God* (New York: Harper & Row, 1968).

6. F. M. Cornford, *From Religion to Philosophy: A Study in the Origins of Western Speculation* (New York: Harper Torchbook, 1957), p. vii. See also William Chase Greene, *Moira: Fate, Good, and Evil in Greek Thought* (Cambridge, Mass.: Harvard University Press, 1944).

7. Lovejoy, *The Great Chain of Being,* p. 5.

Chapter 8: The Meaning of Theological Transformation

1. Margaret Knight, *William James* (London: Penguin Books, 1950), p. 45.

2. *Ibid.* Husserl admits his debt to James in saying that the concept of "horizon" and "horizon consciousness" are derived from James's notion of "fringes." See *Husserliana,* VI, p. 267.

3. See Polanyi, *Personal Knowledge* and *The Tacit Dimension;* and Michael Polanyi and Harry Prosch, *Meaning* (Chicago: University of Chicago Press, 1975).

4. Cp. Husserl's "life-worlds." Hans-Georg Gadamer writes of Husserl: "The concept of 'life-world' is the antithesis of all objectivism. It is an essentially historical concept, which does not refer to a universe of being, to an 'existent world'. . . . But by the life-world is meant . . . the whole in which we exist as historical creatures" (*Truth and Method* [New York: The Seabury Press, 1975], p. 218).

5. Gilbert Ryle, *The Concept of Mind* (New York: Barnes and Noble, Inc., 1949), p. 16.

6. *Ibid.*

7. Charles S. McCoy, "Religious Commitment and Realms of Actuality," in *The Church, the University and Social Policy*, Vol. II (Middletown: Wesleyan University Press, 1969).

8. Thomas S. Kuhn, *The Structures of Scientific Revolution* (Chicago: University of Chicago Press, 1962), pp. 11, 111.

9. *Ibid.*, p. 42.

10. *Ibid.*, (2d ed., 1970), p. 175.

11 We may also discern lesser paradigms within this comprehensive one, e.g. the Thomist paradigm, the Calvinist paradigm, the paradigm of Lutheran orthodoxy, the liberal paradigm, the neoscholastic and neo-orthodox paradigms.

12. Benjamin A. Reist, *Theology in Red, White, and Black* (Philadelphia: The Westminster Press, 1975), pp. 96-97.

Chapter 9: A Federal Paradigm

1. Kuhn, *The Structure of Scientific Revolutions*, p. 42.

2. See Stephen C. Pepper, *World Hypotheses: A Study in Evidence* (Berkeley: University of California Press, 1961); and H. Richard Niebuhr, *The Responsible Self: An Essay in Christian Moral Philosophy* (New York: Harper & Row, 1963), esp. pp. 149-60.

3. Martin Buber, *The Prophetic Faith* (New York: The Macmillan Co., 1949), p. 51.

4. See George E. Mendenhall, *Law and Covenant in Israel and the Ancient Near East* (Pittsburg: Biblical Colloquium, 1954).

5. For example, Johannes Althusius, who published the first federal political philosophy in 1603, studied theology and jurisprudence and taught at Herborn, a center of federal theological thought.

6. Johannes Pedersen, *Israel: Its Life and Culture*, Vols. I-II (London: Oxford University Press, 1926), p. 308.

7. See H. Richard Niebuhr's brilliant treatment of internal and external history in *The Meaning of Revelation*, pp. 65 ff.

8. Alfred North Whitehead, *Adventures of Ideas* (New York: The Macmillan Co., 1933), p. 225.

9. Josiah Royce, *The Problem of Christianity*. 2 vols. (New York: The Macmillan Co., 1913), Vol. II, pp. 140, 142, 169, 247 ff., and 271.

10. H. Richard Niebuhr, *The Responsible Self*, pp. 79-80.

11. Polanyi, *Personal Knowledge*, p. 266.

12. *Ibid.*, pp. 7, 297, 203, 219, and *passim.*

13. Polanyi, *The Tacit Dimension*, pp. 18-19.

14. Kenneth Boulding, *The Image: Knowledge in Life and Society* (Ann Arbor: University of Michigan Press, 1961), p. 14.

15. William James, *The Meaning of Truth* (New York: Longmans, Green, 1909), p. vii.

16. On this issue see the discussion in Richard R. Niebuhr, *Resurrection and Historical Reason.*
17. H. Richard Niebuhr, *The Meaning of Revelation,* p. 191.

Chapter 10: The Gods of Human Believing

1. Kosuke Koyama, *Waterbuffalo Theology* (London: SCM Press, 1974), pp. viii-ix.
2. Luckmann, *The Invisible Religion,* pp. 26-27.
3. William A. Christian, *Meaning and Truth in Religion* (Princeton: Princeton University Press, 1964), pp. 35-36.
4. For example, see Robinson, *Honest to God,* p. 84: "Perhaps the best way to define 'religious' would be to ask, for instance, what is the difference between a religious film and a Christian film. Most people would without thinking tend to equate the two."
5. William James, *The Varieties of Religious Experience.* (New York: The Macmillan Co., 1902), p. 27.
6. Wilfred Cantwell Smith, *The Meaning and End of Religion: A New Approach to the Religious Traditions of Mankind* (New York: Mentor Books, 1964). We must beware of those who follow Durkheim's dictum that "religion is, first and foremost, a system of ideas," and reduce religion to symbol systems. Religion is first lived and only secondarily thought.
7. See Ingo Mörth, *Die gesellschaftliche Wirklichkeit von Religion* (Stuttgart: Verlag W. Kohlhammer, 1978), for an instructive development of a field theory of religion by a sociologist.
8. Paul Tillich, *Systematic Theology,* Vol. I (Chicago: University of Chicago Press, 1951), pp. 11-15.
9. Paul Tillich, *Christianity and the Encounter of the World Religions* (New York: Columbia University Press, 1963), p. 4.
10. H. Richard Niebuhr, *Radical Monotheism and Western Culture* (New York: Harper and Brothers, 1960), p. 119.
11. *Ibid.*
12. Quoted in Davida Foy Crabtree, "Women in Ministry," *A.D.,* December–January, 1978–79, p. 45.
13. Ludwig Feuerbach, *Über das Wesen der Religion.* Sämtliche Werke (Leipzig: O. Wigand, 1851), Band VIII, S. 257.
14. H. Richard Niebuhr, *The Meaning of Revelation,* pp. 93, 109, 138.
15. *Ibid.,* pp. 185, 191.

Chapter 11: Pluralism and Liberation

1. Foreword to Letty M. Russell, *Human Liberation in a Feminist Perspective—A Theology* (Philadelphia: The Westminster Press, 1974), pp. 11, 12.
2. Elsie Thomas Culver traces the all male organization of the church back, at least in part, to its alliance with the Roman Army under Constantine. The Emperor's *quid pro quo* called for "the priests to accompany the troops and help their military morale. In this capacity women were unacceptable." *Women in the World of Religion* (Garden City, N.Y.: Doubleday & Co., 1967), p. 73.

3. Van A. Harvey, "Secularism, Responsible Belief, and the 'Theology of Hope,' " in Frederick Herzog, ed., *The Future of Hope* (New York: Herder and Herder, 1970), pp. 145-46.

4. Frederick Herzog, *Liberation Theology: Liberation in the Light of the Fourth Gospel* (New York: The Seabury Press, 1972), pp. 14, 16, 2-3.

5. James H. Cone, *A Black Theology of Liberation* (Philadelphia: J. B. Lippincott Co., 1970), p. 20.

6. Gayraud Wilmore, *Black Religion and Black Radicalism* (Garden City, N.Y.: Doubleday & Co., 1972), p. 296.

7. See Jürgen Moltmann, *The Crucified God* (New York: Harper & Row, 1974), pp. 329-38.

8. See Johannes Cocceius, *Summa doctrinae de foedere et testamento Dei.* Franeker, 1648, esp. Ch. I; and Jürgen Moltmann, "Geschichtstheologie und pietisches Menschenbild bei Johann Coccejus und Theodor Undereyck," *Evangelische Theologie*, 19, Munich, 1959, S. 343-61.

9. Ernst Bloch, *Atheismus im Christentum: Zur Religion des Exodus und des Reichs* (Hamburg: Rowohlt, 1970), S. 53, 16.

10. Alfred North Whitehead, *Religion in the Making* (New York: The Macmillan Co., 1926), p. 147.

11. Gerhard Sauter, *Zukunft und Verheissung: Das Problem der Zukunft in der gegenwärtigen theologischen und philosophischen Diskussion* (Zurich: Zwingli Verlag, 1965), S. 174.

Chapter 12: A Future for Theology and Ethics

1. Walter Rauschenbusch, *A Theology for the Social Gospel* (New York: The Macmillan Co., 1917), p. 128.

2. Gustavo Gutierrez, *A Theology of Liberation: History, Politics and Salvation.* Maryknoll, N.Y.: Orbis Books, 1973), p. 27, translation slightly altered to avoid sexist language.

3. See Robert McAfee Brown, *Theology in a New Key: Responding to Liberation Themes* (Philadelphia: The Westminster Press, 1978).

4. Moltmann, *The Theology of Hope,* p. 292.

5. Buber, *The Prophetic Faith,* pp. 93-94.

6. Quoted in Moltmann, "Theology as Eschatology" in *The Future of Hope,* p. 41.

7. Chalmers Johnson, *Revolutionary Change* (Boston: Little, Brown, 1966), p. 7. See also Hannah Arendt, *On Revolution* (New York: Viking Press), 1963. Arendt views the Christian conception of history as exclusively Augustinian (p. 20) and ignores the federal understanding. Federal theology views history as divided into periods with decisive differences important for understanding the bourgeois notion of revolution.

8. Guenther Lewy, *Religion and Revolution* (New York: Oxford University Press, 1974), p. 6. Italics of original omitted.

9. Elisabeth Moltmann-Wendel, *Liberty, Equality, Sisterhood* (Philadelphia: Fortress Press, 1978), p. 14.

10. Martin Luther King, Jr., *The Trumpet of Conscience* (New York: Harper & Row, 1968), pp. 74-75.

11. H. Richard Niebuhr, *The Meaning of Revelation,* p. 189.

INDEX

Scripture References

Index of Names and Subjects

WHEN GODS CHANGE

Bifurcation (*see* Dichotomy)
Bloch, Ernst, 39, 216-20, 241, 247
Bohr, Niels, 31-32
Bonhoeffer, Dietrich, 59, 124, 130, 238
Boulding, Kenneth, 184, 245
Brahms, Johannes, 41
Brown, Antoinette, 201
Brown, Robert McAfee, 39, 247
Buber, Martin, 174, 229, 245, 247
Buddha, Buddhism, 67, 75, 80, 138, 142
Bullinger, Heinrich, 120, 155
Bultmann, Rudolf, 26, 29, 124-25, 130, 241

Calhoun, Robert L., 14
Calvin, John, 25, 120, 126
Cao-Dai, 76
Cargo cult, 76
Category mistake, 161-63, 187
Change, 12, 23-41, 47-48, 54, 66-67, 73, 77-78, 104, 132-49, 150-51, 154, 156, 160, 165-67, 206, 210, 215, 219-21, 228-30, 236-40
Changing gods, 17, 26, 32-35, 57, 66-67, 104, 126, 133, 139, 147-49, 158, 189, 197, 215, 219, 224, 227, 229, 239
Christian, William A., 192, 246
Christianity, 23-40, 54, 60, 63, 68-69, 71-75, 84, 110, 113-14, 138, 174, 196-97, 199, 208-9, 211, 213-14, 216, 220, 224, 228-30, 232-33, 238
Christian church, 24, 29, 84, 112, 209
Clement of Alexandria, 112
Cobb, John, 80-81, 242
Cocceius, Johannes, 14, 120, 155, 215, 247
Collingwood, R. G., 182
Colonial mentality, 36, 58
Commitment, 11-12, 32, 46, 56, 67, 70, 89-90, 99-101, 103, 117-18, 133, 140-43, 150-52, 158, 160, 163-64, 174-77, 179, 193-97, 200, 204, 222, 234
Communism, 45, 76
Comprehensive entity, 187-89

Cone, James, 39, 213, 247
Conformity, 45, 51
Confucianism, 75, 142
Congar, Yves, 24
Conversion, 33, 40, 141
Cornford, Francis M., 27, 145, 244
Covenant, 13, 32-36, 38, 58, 73, 79, 83, 99, 100-102, 146-48, 155, 156-58, 160-61, 173-80, 184-85, 188-89, 191, 195-96, 207, 216-20, 228, 238
and liberation, 189
Cox, Harvey, 52, 125, 241, 243
Cratylus, 177
Crick, Francis, 32
Culver, Elsie Thomas, 246
Curie, Marie, 31

d'Arcy, M. C., 242
Darwin, Charles, 32
Demythologize, 31, 67, 91, 124
Descartes, René, 120, 179
Destiny, 145, 236-38
Dewey, John, 52, 155
Dichotomy, 27, 57, 62, 71, 78, 94-96, 109, 114, 119-21, 123, 131, 153-58, 160
Being/appearance, 56, 158
Church/world, 114-15
Essence/existence, 29, 56, 158
Faith/reality, 57, 158
Inner/outer, 95, 119-20
Noumenal/phenomenal, 29, 57, 119-20, 158
Reality/experience, 158
Sacred/secular, 125, 158
Subject/object, 29, 56, 95, 119-20, 153-55, 158, 160, 180
Substance/accident, 29, 56, 158
Theoretical/practical, 29, 57, 121-22
Discovery, 204-6
Driver, Tom F., 129, 244
Durkheim, Émile, 107, 202
Durrell, Lawrence, 92
Dylan, Bob, 134

Ebeling, Gerhard, 71, 114, 242, 243
Ecumenical, 30, 62
Einstein, Albert, 31, 163

INDEX

Eliade, Mircea, 134, 244
Epistemology, 179-84 (*see also* Knowledge, knowing)
Covenantal/federal, 13, 180-81, 183-84
Dyadic/triadic, 179-82
Equality, 13, 51
Ethics, 12-14, 32, 36-37, 40-41, 58, 77, 89, 128-29, 140-41, 148, 222, 227-28, 236

Faith, 11-12, 14, 36-37, 40, 45-47, 52-53, 55-57, 60-62, 66, 71-73, 77, 79, 88, 112, 122, 137-39, 141, 151, 153, 155, 157-58, 165, 169, 189, 193, 199-201, 204, 206, 210, 213-16, 218, 224, 228-29, 231, 236, 240
 Christian, 36-41, 60, 63, 71, 111-13, 152, 172, 176, 199, 238
 Jewish, 60, 63, 11-13, 152, 170-71, 238
Federal, federalism, 35, 53, 77-78, 120, 155, 171, 216, 233 (*see also* Covenant *and* Paradigm, federal)
 derivation from *foedus*, covenant, 171
Fenton, John Y., 244
Feuerbach, Ludwig, 17, 122-23, 126, 202-4, 229-30, 246
Feyerabend, Paul, 49
Fletcher, Joseph, 128, 244
Forell, George W., 242
Freedom, 39, 214, 226, 230-31, 238-39
Freud, Sigmund, 202

Gadamer, Hans-Georg, 244
Gandhi, Mahatma, 142, 235
Garrigou-Lagrange, Reginald, 25
Gerhard, Johann, 38
Gestalt psychology, 155, 158-59
Gibbs, Willard, 31, 155, 162
Global, globalization, 12-14, 25-27, 30-32, 36, 41, 43-45, 48, 50, 52, 56, 64, 74-75, 80, 82, 104, 109, 112, 117-19, 129, 153, 155-56, 165, 171, 210, 224, 227-28, 233, 237

God, 11, 13-14, 18-22, 26, 29, 31, 33-39, 46, 58, 60, 67-68, 71-72, 77-79, 88, 92, 101-6, 107, 114-15, 121-22, 126, 130-31, 133, 143-49, 156, 158, 172, 178, 189, 191, 198-202, 204-5, 207-8, 215-17, 219, 221-25, 228, 230, 237-40
 as discovery, 204-6
 as projection, 202-5
 as revelation, 205-7
 death of, 26, 31, 57, 67, 108, 124-29
 human meaning for, 11, 198-203
gods, 11-13, 21, 25-26, 32-36, 38, 43, 46, 52, 54, 57, 65-77, 84, 91, 103-4, 107, 115, 133-34, 139, 150, 158, 169, 176, 189-90, 192-93, 199-201, 203, 206, 215, 218, 223, 229, 237, 239-40
 believed-in, 11-12, 33, 37, 46-47, 56, 68, 77, 102, 106, 132, 140-41, 150, 156, 190-92, 217
Gogarten, Friedrich, 130
Graduate Theological Union, 14, 62-63
Greene, William Chase, 244
Gutierrez, Gustavo, 226, 247

Hamilton, William, 129, 244
Hare Krishna, 65, 75
Harnack, Adolf von, 24-25, 30-31, 123
Hartshorne, Charles, 221
Harvey, Van A., 210, 247
Hegel, G. W. F., 48, 122-23, 126, 147, 216
Heidegger, Martin, 95-96, 130, 221
Heraclitus, 145
Heretical movements, 76
Herzog, Frederick, 211, 247
Hinduism, 75, 138, 142
History, 24, 29, 34-36, 38-40, 47, 49, 51, 58, 60, 64, 74, 77-79, 81, 86, 89, 92, 101-6, 146, 154-55, 160, 162, 172, 177-78, 180, 186, 190-91, 193, 195, 210, 213-15, 217, 219-

INDEX

INDEX